The Breakdown
of Democratic Regimes
CHILE

The Breakdown of Democratic Regimes, edited by Juan J. Linz and Alfred Stepan, is available in separate paperback editions:

The Breakdown of Democratic Regimes:
Crisis, Breakdown, and Reequilibration
by Juan J. Linz

The Breakdown of Democratic Regimes: Europe
edited by Juan J. Linz and Alfred Stepan

The Breakdown of Democratic Regimes: Latin America
edited by Juan J. Linz and Alfred Stepan

The Breakdown of Democratic Regimes: Chile
by Arturo Valenzuela

The Breakdown
of Democratic Regimes

CHILE

Arturo Valenzuela

The Johns Hopkins University Press

Baltimore and London

The Johns Hopkins University Press, Baltimore, Maryland, 21218
The Johns Hopkins Press Ltd., London

Originally published, 1978
Second printing, 1980
Third printing, 1982

Library of Congress Cataloging in Publication Data

Valenzuela, Arturo, 1944–
    The breakdown of democratic regimes, Chile.

    Includes index.
    1. Chile—Politics and government—1920–
I. Title.
JL2611.V3   320.9′83′064   78–589
ISBN 0–8018–2010–3 pbk.

Contents

Editors' Preface
and Acknowledgments

How and why democratic regimes break down are the central questions addressed by the contributors to this volume.[1] Such breakdowns have long preoccupied social scientists. However, much of the existing literature on the subject has focused attention on the emergence of nondemocratic political forces or the underlying structural strains that lead to the collapse of democratic institutions.[2] Implicitly if not explicitly, the impression often given by such works is that of the virtual inevitability of the breakdown of the democratic regimes under discussion. While recognizing the scholarly legitimacy and analytic utility of studying antidemocratic movements and structural strains, we have addressed a somewhat different aspect of the breakdown of democratic regimes.

Given the tragic consequences of the breakdown of democracy in countries such as Germany, Spain, and Chile, we believed it intellectually and politically worthwhile to direct systematic attention to the dynamics of the political process of breakdown. In particular, we felt it important to analyze the behavior of those committed to democracy, especially the behavior of the incumbent democratic leaders, and to ask in what ways the actions or nonactions of the incumbents contributed to the breakdown under analysis. Did the prodemocratic forces have available to them other options that might have alleviated the crisis of democracy? Was the breakdown of democracy indeed inevitable? A closely related concern of the participants was the endeavor to abstract from the historical record recurrent patterns, sequences, and crises involved in the dynamic process of breakdown.

This publication has a long and complex history. Juan J. Linz's involvement with the question of the breakdown of democracy began with his concern with the fate of Spanish democracy, a fate that affected him as a child in Spain and as a citizen. Linz's reading of the monumental work on the breakdown of the Weimar Republic by Karl Dietrich Bracher led him to ask broad theoretical questions, which he explored with Daniel Bell at Columbia University in the mid-1960s. Linz and Alfred Stepan met at Columbia during this period, when Stepan was beginning to write a dissertation on the breakdown of democracy in Brazil, a process he had seen at first hand while writing articles in Latin America for the *Economist*. Other contributors who were at

Columbia University at the same time included Paolo Farneti, Peter Smith, Arturo Valenzuela, and Alexander Wilde.

In order to encourage scholarly exchange on the political aspects of the breakdown of democracy, a panel was organized under the auspices of the Committee on Political Sociology. This panel met at a number of sessions at the Seventh World Congress of Sociology, held at Varna, Bulgaria, in 1970. Before the congress, Linz circulated a short paper titled "The Breakdown of Competitive Democracies: Elements for a Model," which became the focus of discussion by the members of the panel engaged in studies of individual countries and attending the congress. Among the contributors to the complete hardcover edition of this volume presenting initial drafts of the papers at Varna were Erik Allardt on Finland, Paolo Farneti on Italy, Rainer Lepsius on Weimar Germany, Juan Linz on Spain, Walter Simon on Austria, Peter Smith on Argentina, Alfred Stepan on Brazil, and Alexander Wilde on Colombia. Arend Lijphart was a stimulating commentator.[3]

After fruitful exchanges at Varna, we dispersed with the firm commitment to continue working on the project and to hold a conference in a few years focusing on the comparative and theoretical aspects of our work. In order to introduce other important cases and different perspectives, Stepan encouraged Guillermo O'Donnell to write on the crisis of democracy in Argentina in the decade after the fall of Perón, and Julio Cotler and Daniel Levine to discuss the Peruvian and Venezuelan cases. After the overthrow of Allende in Chile, the editors invited Arturo Valenzuela to analyze the tragic events leading to the end of democracy in Chile.

With the generous support of the Concilium of International and Area Studies of Yale University, and the Joint Committee on Latin America of the Social Science Research Council and the American Council of Learned Societies, the augmented group met at Yale University in December 1973, at a conference chaired by Linz and Stepan, by then both members of the Yale faculty. At this meeting the papers presented benefited from the able suggestions of Douglas Chalmers, Edward Malefakis, and Eric Nordlinger, who acted as discussants. At the end of the conference the participants decided to revise their work in the light of one another's findings and the collective discussion of areas of similarity and dissimilarity. A year at the Institute for Advanced Study in Princeton allowed Linz to revise his introduction and maintain contact with the co-authors.

Despite the groups's interest in underlying, recurrent patterns of breakdown, there has been no attempt to force individual contributors into the procrustean bed of the editors' own thinking. The reader will discover important differences in the authors' intellectual orientations, which grew in part out of the diversity of the democracies studied and reflect in part genuine differences of opinion on the relative weight to be attached to political forces, even after these forces had been given due consideration by all contributors.

It should be stressed that this volume is an initial social scientific effort at middle-level generalizations about complex historical reality. Such a work is, of course, never a substitute for fundamental historical studies of individual cases; rather, it builds upon such studies and, we hope, draws the attention of historians to more generalized propositions, propositions they can in turn pursue further in their own work. Although we are concerned with middle-level generalizations, it is the editors' view that the historicity of macro-political processes precludes the highly abstract generalizing of ahistorical social scientific models of the type susceptible to computer simulations and applicable to all past and any future cases. It is our hope, nevertheless, that scholars interested in developing more formal models may build on our work and incorporate into their models the complex realities here discussed. At this stage of the analysis our collective attention to the political dynamics of the breakdown of democracies has brought to light a number of recurring elements which are discussed at length in Linz's introductory essay. The independent contributions made to breakdowns by political incumbents is a theme that emerges in almost all the papers and has justified our attention to this aspect of the problem, an aspect all too often overlooked. Indeed, in reference to the democratic breakdown in many if not most of the cases analyzed, the editors concur with the remark made by the great German historian, Friedrich Meinecke, upon hearing of the appointment of Hitler to the chancellorship: "This was not necessary."

The individual studies shed new light on some of the most historically important cases of breakdown of democracy, such as Germany, Italy, Spain, and Chile. In addition, some of the less well-known cases forcefully illustrate hitherto neglected aspects of the question of the survival of democracy. Daniel Levine's study of Venezuela examines a fascinating case of political learning. Ten years after the breakdown in Venezuela in 1948, many of the institutional participants in the breakdown—the church, the army, the political parties—consciously and successfully devised strategies to avoid such a breakdown when a new attempt to forge democratic institutions began in 1958. Alexander Wilde's discussion of the reequilibration of Colombian democracy in the 1950s also shows how political learning was crucial for the construction of a consociational democracy. The chapter by Risto Alapuro and Erik Allardt discusses the little-known case of Finland, in which, despite intense conflict, the process of breakdown described in other chapters was avoided. The analysis of nonoccurrence as well as of occurrence increased our understanding of the breakdown process.

With the publication of this project, many of the contributors are turning their attention to closely related issues that loom large on the scholarly agenda. High priority for further work along these lines should now be given to the analysis of the conditions that lead to the breakdown of authoritarian regimes, to the process of transition from authoritarian to democratic regimes, and especially to the political dynamics of the consolidation of postauthoritarian democracies.

The editors want to thank The Johns Hopkins University Press for its help in publishing a project of such large intellectual scope and sheer physical size as this one. We want to give special thanks to Henry Tom, the social sciences editor of the Press, for his great assistance. The project would not have arrived in the reader's hands without extensive copy editing. Jean Savage and Victoria Suddard helped in the early stages of copy editing.

Yale University

JUAN J. LINZ
ALFRED STEPAN

NOTES

1. An extensive discussion of the definition of democracy and the criteria for the selection of cases is found in Juan Linz's introductory essay, entitled *The Breakdown of Democratic Regimes: Crisis, Breakdown, and Reequilibration*. This essay is also available separately as a Johns Hopkins University Press paperback.
2. Much of this literature is discussed in the work by Linz just cited.
3. The crisis of democracy in Portugal in the 1920s, France in the 1950s, Peru and Greece in the 1960s, and the continuing conflict in Northern Ireland were also discussed in papers presented by Herminio Martins, Steven Cohn, David Chaplin, Charles Moskos, and Richard Rose, respectively. Conflicting obligations did not permit them to continue with the project. Richard Rose developed his paper in a somewhat different direction and published it separately as a book, *Governing without Consensus: An Irish Perspective* (Boston: Beacon Press, 1971).

Introduction

On the morning of 11 September 1973, jet aircraft of the Chilean Air Force bombed and strafed La Moneda, the palace of the president and the most vivid symbol of Chile's historic institutions. The smoldering debris marked the downfall of Salvador Allende, a Socialist who had firmly believed he could lead his country down the path of greater social justice within the framework of democratic, pluralist, and libertarian traditions. Allende's tragic death, on the ruins of his experiment, marked not only the demise of the Popular Unity government but also the violent breakdown of one of the world's oldest democracies. What happened? Why did political institutions much admired around the globe cease to function?

Coups d'état and military rule, common in other Latin American countries, had been almost completely absent in Chile since the 1830s. From that date Chilean elites had been able to fashion a viable set of institutions which permitted the vast majority of Chilean presidents to serve out their terms and make way for their duly elected successors.[1]

That process was facilitated by the fact that Chilean elites did not divide sharply along social and economic lines. Both the traditional landed elites and the newer mining and commercial interests shared a similar stake in Chile's export economy.[2] Divisions emerged primarily over a series of issues related to the expansion of a centralized secular state. By the mid-1850s, local notables and the church had become increasingly alarmed over the central state's penetration of society. The revolt of 1891 was aimed in large measure at returning autonomy to local leaders.[3] Though the revolt undermined presidential authority, it did not destroy the commitment to representative institutions. The Parliament grew in prestige and influence, in turn contributing to the expansion of stable political party networks. Unlike their neighbors in Argentina, by the turn of the century Chilean middle-class parties had become full participants in the governing process. They emerged before the development of a strong bureaucracy and the push for mass participation and became the key brokers tying political clienteles to the emerging state apparatus.[4]

Though parties were instrumental in channeling and controlling mobilization and moderating political conflict among elites, it must be stressed that

This study was first presented at the conference on "Breakdowns and Crises of Democratic Regimes," Yale University, 10–15 December 1973.

Chilean democracy was hardly characterized by social peace. Large portions of the population were excluded from active citizenship and the incipient working-class movement was at times brutally repressed.[5] Political democracy never really meant social democracy, as sharp inequality and a meager standard of living for the vast majority of the population continued to be important features of Chilean society. Nevertheless, the openness of the rules of competitive politics and the legitimacy of institutions did allow for the rise of Marxist electoral parties with roots in the urban and mining proletariat. In turn, the support of the Left gave middle-class parties the necessary impetus to achieve control of the government and to bring about a whole array of reforms that benefited the working class. The rise of a strong Left clearly polarized Chilean politics, but the Marxist parties abided by Chilean rules of the game, gaining considerable electoral strength by mid-century.[6] In the 1960s significant reforms, particularly in the rural areas, further consolidated the growing gains of previously excluded elements.

The purpose of this study is to analyze why and how Chilean democracy broke down. In so doing, it will describe in as much detail as strictly necessary the political events during the period just before the coup d'état—stressing the positions of the key actors and the impact of political as well as economic developments on the final outcome. The study, however, cannot restrict itself merely to a review of the important events in the months before the breakdown. A description of the Allende years must be preceded by a careful analysis of the principal characteristics of Chilean politics at mid-century. Only with a prior understanding of the main features of the political system is it possible to draw on the Chilean experience to make meaningful observations about the functioning and crises of competitive democratic regimes. This is true for three reasons. In the first place, without knowledge of the nature of the system which broke down, it is difficult to judge whether the breakdown constitutes a fundamental crisis of regime or is merely another in the series of recurring "crises" which continually characterize some political systems. Secondly, a description of the system is a prerequisite to a full understanding of the principal factors or developments which are at the root of the breakdown. Is it underlying stress in the political system itself which precipitates or exacerbates the crisis? Or is the crisis primarily the result of socioeconomic difficulties around the time of military intervention? Alternatively, is the crisis due to the mistakes and irresponsibility of key political personalities? If several factors are involved, how do they relate to one another? It follows that it is only with a thorough consideration of the principal dimensions of the political system that one can ascertain the extent to which they define or shape the actions of individuals and groups, leaders and followers. In the final analysis, we need to know what range there is for human choice. To what extent were the actors in the human drama destined to live out their fate—or to what extent could they have chosen a different denouement?

It soon became clear in completing the research for this project that while the background of the Chilean system could be presented in essentially static terms, the process of breakdown could only be analyzed in a dynamic fashion. This is the reason for the largely chronological organization of the work. In the fast-moving and changing context of Chilean politics the principal factors and characteristics of the system could change significantly at any point in time. The process was dialectical. Actions by one set of actors within the framework of rules and institutions at time A were followed by counteractions by others which not only affected the correlation of forces but changed the very rules of the game for time B. The system which had existed in 1971 was a different one after the October 1972 strike and the incorporation of the military into the cabinet. There was also a fundamental change after the March 1973 elections and the 29 June 1973 coup attempt. Unfortunately for those wishing to avoid a much more devastating "fate" than a representative democratic regime, as the system evolved the range of choice was also diminished and the outcome became more and more certain.

It is the principal thesis of this work that the main characteristic of the Chilean system by mid-twentieth century was a marked political polarization. Conflict and confrontation were mediated by a web of institutions and through the verdict of an electoral system which defined the power capabilities of political groups. Polarization was initially restricted to elites; as time went on it became increasingly pervasive. Polarization was aggravated by the loss of a pragmatic Center coalition and the rise of an ideological Center party under the Christian Democrats. Political competition preceded and indeed accelerated class competition. In turn, the economic crisis followed the political crisis, rather than vice versa. Certain characteristics of the Chilean institutional arena, including winner-take-all elections, contributed to a centrifugal tendency (to use Giovanni Sartori's term) which placed great stress on the whole system.

The Chilean case supports Juan Linz's contention that it is not the actions of the extreme forces on the Right and Left per se which have brought down democratic regimes.[7] Certainly their actions were profoundly disruptive and created extraordinary difficulties for those who believed that change could be brought about within traditional institutional parameters. But the extremes were a constant in the political system. The actual breakdown was more the result of the inability of centrist forces—of democrats on both sides of the divided political system—to see the logic of escalating crisis, or for that matter, foresee the dire consequences of a repressive authoritarian regime. As group stakes, narrow stakes, prevailed, the room for maneuvering was drastically reduced. The outcome that all secretly dreaded, but refused to face, came to pass.

This study challenges some fashionable assumptions about the Chilean case and democratic regimes in general. The fact that centrist elements did not succeed in structuring agreements to save the system does not mean that the outcome was inevitable. The constraints were often formidable and became increasingly so. But there was room for action to save the system at critical junctures. It is a myth that the outcome would have been different had Allende taken the advice of the maximalists within his own coalition and sought to accelerate a violent class confrontation. Such a strategy would merely have hastened the coup d'état by undermining the traditional system even sooner. It is also a myth that change and progressive policies would have been impossible within the framework of ongoing institutions. Certainly the kinds of fundamental transformations that some sectors sought would have been impossible. But they would have been extraordinarily difficult to achieve, given the short time span, in any regime, even the most progressive. The sad irony is that today not only has the hope of fundamental transformation vanished for the foreseeable future, but much of the genuine progress which Chile made over the years has been severely undermined. The worst myth of all is that the working class in Chile had not made any real progress. Much blood and suffering went into the accumulation of the victories of the Chilean working class. Though narrow in scope, those victories loom as monumental ones in the context of a regime which today deprives the population of fundamental human rights and has led the country back into the early twentieth century in social rights.

But is is also a myth that democracy is a failure because it inevitably allows for the rise of progressive forces capable of consolidating substantial electoral support. Those who condemn Chilean institutions and procedures for having allowed ''foreign'' influences to enter Chilean political life fail to see how integral those forces were in Chilean society and how great a stake they had in the system. By interpreting the breakdown of democracy as inevitable, these sinister forces can more easily justify the injustices and abuses of the present. This author hopes that other observers, in other times and places, will draw the basic lesson from the Chilean case. Democracy is a system difficult to create, perhaps more difficult to preserve. Given the alternative of authoritarianism, every effort to maintain democracy is well worth the price.

I have benefited greatly from the help of many people in completing this study. My greatest debt is to the many Chilean politicians, officials, and observers who gave freely of their time to tell me their versions of what happened. For many the process of thinking about and remembering what happened in Chile is a painful one. I am deeply grateful for our open and candid conversations which enabled me to piece together aspects of the tragic puzzle, even if incompletely. Several of my sources will, and already have, disagreed strongly with some of the judgments in this study. I am, of course, solely responsible for these judgments.

Interviewees ranged from a former president and former cabinet officers in the Frei and Allende administrations, to ex-middle level leaders such as congressmen, agency heads and sub-heads, and labor leaders, to former municipal and local party officials in Santiago and in a sample of eight communities in southern Chile. In addition the author benefited from numerous conversations with colleagues in Chile, the United States, and Europe who have followed Chilean developments closely for years. The interviews in Chile were conducted in July 1972, February 1974, and during a longer stay in Chile from July 1974 to January 1975. The first part of the study also draws extensively on field research conducted in Chile during 1969. Many of the interviewees requested anonymity. Because of the brutality of repression under the military junta, I have decided for the time being not to reveal the names of those interviewed. At least one of those interviewed was brutally assassinated and others have been arrested or harrassed. Sections of the study which draw primarily from interview sources have been identified. Because so much of the Chilean political debate was reported openly and fully, if not accurately, by the free press, it has been possible to use public sources for the bulk of the study.

I would like to acknowledge publicly the continued guidance which I have received from J. Samuel Valenzuela in the long and arduous process of writing this book. His keen judgment, his genuine concern, and his candid appraisals have been invaluable assets. He shares with me whatever there is of value in this work but is exonerated from any shortcomings. My father, Raimundo Valenzuela, also provided indispensable encouragement. His incisive reading of an earlier draft of the manuscript and his encyclopedic knowledge of Chilean affairs saved me from numerous serious errors. From the very inception of this project, Juan Linz and Alfred Stepan have provided help and support. The Chilean case reveals how accurate and perceptive were many of Juan Linz's generalizations about the nature of crisis in democratic regimes. Alfred Stepan not only provided intellectual advice but also ensured that the project of which this study is a part reached publication. Henry Y. K. Tom of the Johns Hopkins University Press has been patient and understanding.

The completion of this book would have been difficult without the generous support of the Committee on Latin America of the Social Science Research Council, which enabled me to spend several months in Chile in 1974, and the continuous support of the Duke University Research Council, which made it possible to complete much of the quantitative analysis.

The Breakdown
of Democratic Regimes
CHILE

1.
Chilean Politics at Mid-Century

The Party System

Students of Latin American politics have often observed that Chile's political system was significantly different from those found on the rest of the continent. As Federico Gil has noted, in his basic work on Chilean politics, this distinctiveness was due in large measure to Chile's party system, "where political forces [were] clearly and distinctly aligned, as in many European countries." As Gil says, "the resemblance of the Chilean party system to that of much of Europe, and particularly to the system which existed in France during the Third and Fourth republics, is striking."[1] Chile's party system was everywhere, not only determining the political recruitment process for important national posts but also structuring contests in such diverse institutions as government agencies, professional and industrial unions, neighborhood organizations, and even local high schools. Parties were so much a feature of national life that in a survey conducted in Santiago, only 22.2 percent of Santiago residents felt parties could be dispensed with in governing the country.[2]

An important characteristic of the Chilean party system was its high degree of competitiveness. In the 1930s there were over thirty party organizations. Changes in the electoral law and the consolidation of party strengths had reduced that number to ten by 1970.[3] Despite the decline in the number of parties, no Chilean party has received more than 30 percent of the vote in either a congressional or a municipal election since the adoption of the 1925 constitution.[4] The only exceptions occurred in the 1965 and 1967 congressional and municipal elections, in which the Christian Democrats obtained 42.3 percent and 35.6 percent respectively, only to see their percentage of the vote decline in subsequent contests. These national figures mask the fact that parties structured competition even in the smallest and most backward municipalities. Analysis of aggregate data shows that the fractionalization of the vote did not vary much, controlling either for size or level of socioeconomic development of communities. Furthermore, the contest for local office was as intense and competitive as the contest for the national legislature.[5]

In 1970, this system was composed of five major parties and several minor parties spanning the ideological spectrum. The Right comprised the National party, formed in 1966 by a fusion of the traditional Conservatives and Liberals in an effort to overcome a steady erosion of their electoral fortunes. Though committed to the Chilean rules of the democratic game (which they had helped to shape), the Nationals were also clearly committed to the prevailing Chilean socioeconomic system, which had given their leaders positions of wealth and status in society.[6] The Left in Chile was dominated by the Communist and Socialist parties. The former was the largest Communist party in Latin America outside Cuba, and it adhered closely to Moscow's directions. The Socialist party, which had been racked by dissension since its creation, had a more heterogeneous base than the Communists. After years of bitter rivalry, interrupted by occasional agreements, the two Marxist parties instituted an alliance in 1956 known as the Frente de Acción Popular (FRAP), which backed Salvador Allende's unsuccessful candidacy for the presidency in 1958. The FRAP served as the immediate forerunner of the Popular Unity coalition, which in 1970 finally succeeded in electing Allende to the nation's highest office.[7]

The Center was occupied by the anticlerical Radicals—once the dominant party of the Chilean political system—which saw its role diminish markedly, first with the rise of Carlos Ibañez's populism in the 1950s and then with the rise of the Christian Democratic party in the 1960s. The Christian Democrats surged into prominence as a reform movement of the Center, advocating a "revolution in liberty." Fear of Allende's Marxist supporters contributed to a heavy Christian Democratic vote in the 1964 presidential election. However, the party's strength quickly eroded as both Right and Left increased their share of the electorate toward the end of Eduardo Frei's term in office.[8]

It is apparent that Chile's party system was not only highly competitive but also highly polarized. A substantial portion of the electorate either supported parties committed to a radical transformation of the social and political structures or parties vehemently opposed to any change in the status quo. The 1958 Santiago survey cited earlier revealed that 31.4 percent of the respondents classified themselves as rightists, and 24.5 percent classified themselves as leftists. A smaller number, 17.8 percent, placed themselves in the center of the political spectrum, while a quarter of the respondents gave no specific answer. As table 1 shows, with the exception of the small upper-class group, all of the class categories showed evidence of significant polarization. James Prothro and Patricio Chaparro have compared the Hamuy findings with more recent survey data and concluded that this distribution of public opinion on a Left-Right continuum remained markedly stable from 1958 to 1970.[9] The polarization of Chilean politics is also clearly evident in the verdict of the electorate. Under the proportional representation system of the 1925 constitution, the Socialist and Communist parties made steady headway, particularly

Table 1. Self-identification of Chileans as to Political Preference and Social Class

SOCIAL CLASS

Political Preference	Upper N	Upper %	Upper-Middle N	Upper-Middle %	Lower-Middle N	Lower-Middle %	Working N	Working %	No Answer N	No Answer %	Total N	Total %
Right	11	78.6	67	33.0	98	32.8	60	29.4	17	54.8	253	31.4
Center	3	21.4	63	31.0	59	19.7	19	9.6	0	0.0	144	17.8
Left	0	0.0	37	18.2	58	19.4	100	31.1	3	9.7	198	24.5
Other	0	0.0	4	2.0	4	1.3	3	0.7	1	3.2	12	1.5
No answer	0	0.0	32	15.8	80	26.8	78	29.2	10	32.3	200	24.8
Total in sample	14		203		299		250		31		807	

SOURCE: International Data Library and Reference Service, Survey Research Center, "1958 Presidential Election Survey in Santiago, Chile" (University of California, Berkeley).

in urban and mining communities, while the Right continued to dominate Chile's backward rural areas and maintain the allegiance of many groups of the growing middle-class sector. Over the last thirty years the Right obtained an average of about 30 percent of the vote to the Left's 20 percent—though by 1973 increasing support for the Left had reversed those proportions. Table 2 shows divisions of the Chilean electorate in all congressional elections from 1937 to 1973, underscoring the continued polarization. The table shows that parties of the Center surged at the expense of both Right and Left; but, except in the 1965 contest, they never received more than 50 percent of the suffrage. Over time, three important centrist tendencies can be noted. The first was that of the Radical party, which dominated Chilean politics from 1938 to 1952. Though it allied with the Left to gain the presidency in the 30s and 40s, it became increasingly concerned over the rising strength of the Communists, particularly after the 1947 municipal election.[10] As a result, the Communist party was declared illegal and the Radical party veered sharply to the Right. This event, and many years in the presidential palace, took its toll on the increasingly weak centrist party.[11] The Radicals were replaced as the Center by the dramatic ascendancy of former-president Carlos Ibañez, who won the presidency in 1952 at the head of a disparate coalition of groups ranging from the radical wing of the Socialist party to elements tied closely to the Chilean Nazi movement. Ibañez's centrist movement, however, did not survive his own directionless administration, and by the end of his term the Left, including the now-legal Communist party, had regained its electoral strength.[12] With the demise of the Ibañez coalition, the Christian Democrats became the new centrist movement, this time drawing primarily on support from the Right. As noted above, by the end of the 1960s its impressive support had also withered.

Table 2. Percentage of Vote Received by Parties on the Right, Center, and Left in Chilean Congressional Elections, 1937 to 1973

| | DIPUTADO ELECTIONS | | | | | | | | | |
| | Percentage of Total Vote | | | | | | | | | |
Party	1937	1941	1945	1949	1953	1957	1961	1965	1969	1973	Mean
Right (Conservative, Liberal, National after 1965)	42.0	31.2	43.7	42.0	25.3	33.0	30.4	12.5	20.0	21.3	30.1
Center (Radical, Falangist, Christian Democrats, Agrarian Laborist)	28.1	32.1	27.9	46.7	43.0	44.3	43.7	55.6	42.8	32.8	39.7
Left (Socialist, Communist)	15.4	33.9	23.1	9.4	14.2	10.7	22.1	22.7	28.1	34.9	21.5
Other	14.5	2.8	5.3	1.9	17.5	12.0	3.8	9.2	9.1	11.0	8.7

SOURCE: Dirección del Registro Electoral, Santiago, Chile.

Giovanni Sartori, drawing on his studies of Italian politics, has stressed the importance of polarization and the role of centrist parties in understanding the dynamics of a multi-party system.[13] Sartori argues that in a highly polarized context, with a clearly defined Right and Left commanding substantial percentages of the electorate, the principal drive of the political system will be centrifugal. This means that a polarized system has a tendency to move toward the extremes—toward greater divisions in the society. Unlike party systems which have avoided the emergence of clearly opposing tendencies, a polarized party system has no strong centripetal drive—no dominant centrist consensus. Ironically, polarized systems do have Center poles occupied by one or more parties. However, Sartori argues, under such circumstances the Center does not represent a significant political tendency in itself but tends to be composed of fragments emanating from both the Left and the Right poles. Sartori notes that the "center is mainly a feedback of the centrifugal drives which predominate in the system" and is "more a negative convergence, a sum of exclusions, than a positive agency of instigation."[14] Sartori's analysis is extremely helpful in understanding the Chilean case, because it explains the repeated surge of centrist movements in Chilean politics which rose at the expense of both Right and Left. Since these centrist movements only minimally represented a viable centrist tendency and were in fact primarily reflections of the erosion of the two extreme poles, they have crumbled, only to make way for a new centrist coalition. The instability of centrist movements, in turn, contributed to difficulties in structuring common public policies because of the resulting fragility of centrist consensus at the decision-making level. The erosion of centrist consensus would accelerate dramatically during the Allende years and contribute directly to the crisis culminating in regime breakdown.

It is important to stress that the polarized party system had a different impact in Chile's presidential system than it did in the Italian parliamentary system which Sartori studies. Despite competitiveness, polarization, and the instability of centrist options, the government in Chile was not in danger of "falling" if it failed to gain, or lost, majority support in the legislature. By the same token, coalitions, which were formed in the legislature after a parliamentary election in Italy, had to be structured before the presidential election in Chile. As noted above, no single party or tendency was capable of winning the presidency on its own. Either the presidency was won by a small plurality or shifting centrist groups became the key to the election. Candidates of the Center were elected with support from the Left in the presidential elections of 1938 and 1946; with support from the Right in 1932 and 1964; and with support from both sides in 1952. Only on two occasions during that period did the presidency go to a candidate representing the Right or Left; in 1958, when the Conservative Jorge Alessandri was elected, and in 1970, when the Marxist Salvador Allende won. In both cases the poles rejected compromise and the parties of the Center mistakenly thought they would succeed on their own. The Chilean political system was able to cope successfully with Alessandri's rightist presidency, for soon centrist groups joined his administration. As will be seen below, a centrist coalition was never successfully structured during the Allende years.

Since preelection coalitions were constituted primarily for electoral reasons, in an atmosphere of considerable political uncertainty, they tended to disintegrate after a few months of the new administration. Ideological disputes were often at the root of coalition changes, as partisans of one formula would resist the proposals of other partisans. But narrow political considerations were also important. The president could not succeed himself, and it soon became apparent to the leadership of other parties in his own coalition that they could best improve their fortunes in succeeding municipal and congressional elections by dissociating themselves from the difficulties of incumbency in a society fraught with economic problems. For in the final analysis, only by proving electoral strength in subsequent elections in which parties ran on their own could a party demonstrate its value to future presidential coalitions. Erosion of preelection coalitions inevitably led to new temporary alliances with parties and groups willing to provide congressional and general political support to the executive in exchange for presidential concessions. President Gonzalez Videla turned to the Liberals after he dissolved his alliance with the Communists. Carlos Ibañez also turned to the Right when he accepted the support of the Conservative party at a critical point in the mid-1950s. President Alessandri, elected by the Right, was finally forced to make an agreement with the centrist Radicals to maintain a workable administration. Elections were clearly characterized by the politics of outbidding, since the fate of a government did not hang on a lost vote. Parties went out of their way to criticize incumbents and would seize on every inflationary increase, every incident of police repression, every allegation of partisan or corrupt practice in an effort to pave the way for a better showing at the polls. The rhetoric of the party-controlled press and of the skilled orators of the party leadership occasionally reached frenzied proportions. In such an atmosphere, centrist parties with basically pragmatic orientations, who shifted from support to opposition and then again to support of an incumbent, suffered politically. Perhaps even more than in a parliamentary system, the forces of "polarized pluralism" contributed to further polarization with their centrifugal tendencies.

Paradoxically, in light of this discussion of competitiveness and polarization, the Chilean party system was also characterized by the central importance of particularistic transactions involving small rewards and payoffs for political support. Elected officials from all groups and factions spent a major part of their waking moments obtaining pensions for widows, jobs for school teachers, higher salary increases for unions or trade associations, bridges for local municipalities, and a host of other favors either by acting directly or by serving as intermediaries before the complex and ubiquitous state bureaucracy. In Chile, the advent of the politics of ideology and program did not erode the particularisitc politics of earlier years; it merely added a new dimension to the political system.

In analytical terms, we can think of the party system as being divided into two distinct arenas.[15] In the central arena, with its primary locus in the capital city, major controversies over matters such as redistributive legislation, the survival of presidential cabinets, and the structuring of new presidential alliances clearly predominated. The principal actors were ministers, high-level bureaucrats, party officials, youth leaders, and congressmen. Many of these leaders owed their careers either directly or indirectly to support from the small group of party activists and militants who controlled party organizations. Some national figures, such as Eduardo Frei and Salvador Allende, operated almost exclusively in this arena, paying little attention to the more mundane side of politics. Others, including most congressmen not occupying major party roles, straddled both arenas, often with considerable difficulty.

By contrast, in the local arena, at the grass-roots of the political system, payoffs and political favors were the primary stuff of politics. Indeed, much of the Chilean style of electoral campaigning depended on the face to face contact between candidates and supporters aimed at translating particularistic favors into votes and party loyalty. Candidates for congressional offices with large constituencies made widespread use of lower-level brokers such as municipal councillors in consolidating their own support. In return, local brokers could expect that the congressman or senator would help to satisfy his own client's needs, either directly, by acting as an intermediary with the bureaucracy, or by congressional action. The local arena was not restricted only to individualistic demands. It also included the demands of a multitude of organized groups, most of which had close party ties. In Chile, private sector groups ranged from professional associations, business organizations, and student and youth groups to labor unions, church groups, and local neighborhood councils.

Most of these groups were organized into national confederations. For example, professional societies created the Confederation of Professional Associations, which was mandated to defend the interest of all university-trained professionals before the government and the public at large. The powerful Society for Industrial Advancement (SOFOFA) included many regional industrial groups as well as individual members and claimed to represent most of Chilean private industry.[16] Labor unions of private and public employees and farm workers were also organized into various national confederations, most of which were in turn affiliated with the *Central Unica de Trabajadores*.[17] The agrarian reform process begun during the Frei administration added a whole new array of rural unions, cooperatives, and *asentamientos* to this vast institutional structure.

Whether it was a particular business seeking tax relief, a union organization seeking the establishment of a pension fund, a professional association after legal recognition, or a municipality after a new dam, political leaders and officials were continuously besieged by an overwhelming number of petitions. Parties were without question the key networks for processing demands, often by channeling them up through different levels of the party hierarchy. As noted above, congressmen were the most important national brokers and were the primary link between the two arenas.[18]

This dual system, with roots in the patron-client politics of the parliamentary republic at the turn of the century, was continually reinforced by the highly centralized nature of the Chilean political and administrative system and the very scarce resources of its weak economy.[19] The system was also reinforced by various aspects of the electoral system, notably the absence of cumulative voting in Chile's modified version of the D'Hondt proportional representation system. Though each party presented a list, which could include as many candidates as there were seats, voters could cast their votes for only one candidate. The total vote for all candidates on each list was used to decide how many seats a particular party could fill. If a party was entitled to one or more seats, those candidates receiving the highest individual vote would take those seats.[20] Candidates were thus running not only against candidates of opposition parties but against candidates on their own party list, attempting to insure the highest plurality. Followers, committed to a party for ideological or traditional reasons, often chose their particular candidate over others on the party slate, depending on his or her ability to deliver the particularistic goods.

In the absence of adequate survey data, it is difficult to ascertain the relative importance of particularistic services and ideological commitments in cementing party loyalty and determining electoral behavior. Undoubtedly, both elements interacted with others, such as traditional party identification and reference group influence, and had differing effects on different voting groups. What is important to stress, given the central role of particularistic transactions in Chilean politics, is that party polarization was not due solely to underlying ideological cleavages in society. A very important factor in shaping and perpetuating continued polarization was the sharp ideological polarization characteristic of the central arena. It was the highly ideological political elites, in control of powerful party organizations, who structured the options of the electorate. Small parties, independent candidates, and fractions of former parties had little chance of surviving. Many citizens were committed to particular options, either because of clientelistic politics, ideological proclivities, or both. For that reason alone, the structuring of new options would have been enormously difficult. What made it virtually impossible to break out of the polarized system was the increased polarization among party activists, who in turn, and in a somewhat circular fashion, further polarized the system at the mass level. Thus, for example, the decline of the Christian Democrats was not due only to loss of support among the populace because the party represented a dubious centrist tendency. It was also reinforced by repeated party splits at the elite level, followed by actual defections by elements who wanted to identify more closely with Marxist parties. This undermined any possibility of capitalizing on the party's fragile strength in order to become a viable Center. The sharp polarization in the 1960s among activists in the Radical party, which made the two principal factions practically indistinguishable from the two extreme poles of the party system and led to the formation of two parties, the Radical and the Radical Democracy parties, helped to preclude any comeback of the Radicals as either a centrist tendency or a Center pole.

This description of the Chilean party system parallels in some respects Duncan MacRae's description of the French system under the Fourth Republic. MacRae maintains that the sharp divisions in French politics were not simply a reflection of sharp societal divisions. Certainly latent divisions existed and exist today in French society, but as MacRae notes, they "constituted a permissive but not sufficient condition for political division." Actual political divisiveness depended on other factors and especially on "the existence of sets of intermediate political leaders divided on national issues, talking of national problems in different terms from one another, and not interpenetrating with one another."[21] In Chile, as in France, the polarized group of activists sought to channel the latent divisions in society with both programmatic and particularistic strategies, reinforcing polarization of the entire system.

The importance of particularistic transactions and the attachment of many voters to parties because of a traditional identification that often spanned several generations helps to explain a final feature of the Chilean party system: its heterogeneous base of support. In turn, the heterogeneous base of support further reinforced the important role of particularistic transactions, as party leaders sought to retain the allegiance of sectors actively being wooed by elements claiming to better represent their interests. Clearly the Socialist and Communist parties received a significant portion of their support from organized working-class elements. This was due to growing class consciousness as well as the simple fact that leftist parties were the first to move in and provide services and benefits to previously disenfranchised urban and mining groups. By the same token, the National party drew the strongest support from the most privileged sectors of society. And yet survey research shows that most parties, particularly the centrist and rightist parties, had cross-class support, drawing substantial votes from both urban and rural low income sectors. Thus Alejandro Portes, in his study of squatter settlements in Santiago in 1969, found that the Christian Democratic party received as much support from low income groups as did the Communists and Socialists combined.[22] The Hamuy survey, conducted in 1958, reported similar findings: a substantial portion of the population in working-class categories supported the Right. And yet the Hamuy data, presented in table 3, also reveal a sizable proportion of university-trained professionals and middle-level managers who were more likely to support the Left than the Right. Only unskilled workers, small businessmen, and managers of large business concerns indicated political leanings more consistent with expected class interests. Aggregate data analysis, while confirming that the Left drew more from working-class sectors and the Right from upper-class groups, also lends support to the finding that much of the support was quite heterogeneous. As table 4 notes, working-class categories did not explain a substantial amount of the variance in party vote for any party, with the exception of the Communists, whose vote was heavily determined by the mining population.[23] These findings further support the notion that polarization in Chile, though channeling and to a great degree reflecting latent societal cleavages, was more directly influenced by the polarization of options as structured by the elites and party militants.

The Institutional Context and the Rules of the Game

Chilean politics was characterized by a highly competitive and polarized party system. In such an atmosphere, centrist consensus was always fragile, and coalitions disintegrated with ease, as parties and groups struggled to

Table 3. Distribution by Occupational Categories of Preference for the Political Right, Center, or Left of a Sample of Chileans in 1958

Political Preference	Domestic Servants		Unskilled Workers		Self-employed Workers		Skilled and Semi-skilled Workers		White-Collar Workers		Small Businessmen		Middle Manager and Professionals		Large Company Managers		Not Ascertained		Total	
	N	%	N	%	N	%	N	%	N	%	N	%	N	%	N	%	N	%	N	%
Right	13	38.2	26	22.4	71	40.1	26	27.1	67	37.7	23	37.7	15	20.5	10	58.8	2	66.7	253	31.4
Center	2	5.9	11	9.5	22	12.4	9	9.4	58	25.2	19	31.1	20	27.4	3	17.6	0	0.0	144	17.8
Left	6	17.6	44	37.9	36	20.3	35	36.5	49	21.3	4	6.6	21	28.8	2	11.8	1	33.3	198	24.5
Other	0	0.0	1	0.9	2	1.1	1	1.0	3	1.3	2	3.3	3	4.1	0	0.0	0	0.0	12	1.5
Other and Not ascertained	13	38.2	34	29.3	46	26.0	25	26.0	53	23.0	13	21.3	14	19.2	2	11.8	0	0.0	200	24.8
Total	34	4.2	116	14.4	177	21.9	96	11.9	230	28.5	61	7.6	73	9.0	17	2.1	3	0.4	807	100.0

SOURCE: International Data Library and Reference Service, Survey Research Center, "1958 Presidential Election Survey in Santiago, Chile," (University of California, Berkeley).

Table 4. Variation in the Vote for Each Major Chilean Party or Alliance in a National and a Local Election Explained by Socioeconomic Indicators (in percentages)

Election	Nationals	Radicals	Christian Democrats	Communists	Socialists
Congressional election of 1969	28.3	8.5	18.5	22.6	9.8
Municipal election of 1967	22.8	13.5	17.1	40.0	12.2

SOURCE: Electoral data from the Dirección del Registro Electoral, Santiago, Chile.
NOTES: N = 287 communes.
Coefficients of determination (R²) expressed in percentage form. All multiple correlation coefficients (R) significant at .001 level.
The independent variables are medical assistance, homes with bathrooms, school attendance, population in industry, population in construction, population in services, population in mining, instruction, and population size. The dependent variables are the percentages of the vote which each party or alliance received in each election and in each commune.

outbid each other in gaining the favor of the electorate. Yet it would be seriously misleading to describe Chilean politics only in terms of parties and groups, leaders and followers. Ideological confrontations and group demands should not obscure the fact that the Chilean political system was also highly institutionalized. Strong governmental institutions played key roles in the public policy-making process, and most relevant political actors accepted the validity of both codified rules and procedures and a host of informal practices which had evolved over generations to rationalize the political process.

The Chilean state consisted of an awesome set of structures and institutions. Even before the election of Salvador Allende to the presidency, the state played a greater role in the nation's economy than it did in the economy of any other Latin American country with the exception of Cuba. By the end of the 1960s direct public investment represented well over 50 percent of all the gross investment, and the state controlled over 50 percent of all credit. Furthermore, the government accounted for 14 percent of the GNP and 13 percent of the economically active population.[24] A state agency, the *Corporación de Fomento de la Producción* (CORFO), owned shares in eighty of the country's most important enterprises and institutions, and majority shares in thirty-nine of the same.[25] Most private groups and institutions were closely regulated by the state and relied on its favorable dispensations. Not only did it chart the course for economic growth and control prices, it also ran the major social security programs and had a dominant role in collective bargaining.

But the important point about the Chilean institutional system is not only its size. The key point is that Chilean politics were not praetorian politics. Unlike the politics of some of its neighbors, Chilean politics did not involve the naked confrontation of political forces, each seeking to maximize its own stakes through direct action in the face of transitory authority structures incapable of guarding, even in the most elementary fashion, the public good.[26] Elected and nonelected officials, if not party militants, were able to put aside the acrimonious verbal assaults of afternoon political rallies and come together to structure compromises during the evening hours, whether in a congressional committee room or over a late meal in a Santiago restaurant. Bitter exchanges on the nature of the Cuban Revolution, the Vietnam War, the exploitation of workers, or copper nationalization gave way to hard-nosed bargaining on the next wage readjustment or budget supplement bill, or a joint strategy to obtain a new hospital for the community of Mulchen. At the same time, powerful state structures, largely insulated from political control and partisan battles, exercised important governmental functions drawing on formal authority and institutional clout. Thus the comptroller general could obtain the arrest of the mayor and all the municipal councillors of the city of Ancud for granting a Christmas bonus from a budget item designated for another purpose;[27] or the *Dirección del Trabajo* could institute a formidable array of rules and procedures for "conciliation" in order to resolve a labor dispute.[28]

It is beyond the scope of this work to provide a detailed description of the Chilean institutional context.[29] However, before turning to a discussion of the "rules of the game," noting the key role of the legislature in the political process, a brief mention of the most prominent institutions is in order.

In addition to the president and Congress, the Chilean constitution specified two additional branches of government, the court system and the *Contraloría General de la República*. The courts had a long tradition of independence from the executive and constituted a bulwark for the protection and interpretation of a highly detailed legal code dedicated in large measure to the preservation of traditional institutions and economic relations. Appointments at all levels of the hierarchy were based on seniority and merit and were determined by the institution itself, as the executive could choose the appointee only from lists submitted to him by the courts. Supreme Court justices were appointed for life, and the court alone had the power to remove judges for malfeasance. Though the court's power of judicial review was limited in comparison to that of the U.S. Supreme Court, the court could declare unconstitutional a legislative act as applied to a specific case.[30]

One of the most unusual branches of the Chilean government was its independent *Contraloría*. An agency with a career staff composed of over 750 civil servants and a director appointed for life, the Contraloría was charged with a variety of functions, ranging from audits of public accounts to ruling on the legality of executive decrees and issuing advisory opinions on the constitutionality of proposed congressional legislation. Unlike the courts, which intervened once litigation was instituted, the Contraloría gave its opinions in response to informal requests by elected officials of opposition groups and private parties. A prestigious organization, the Contraloría commanded respect from most Chilean civil servants, who feared its scrupulous championship of legalism and frugality, sometimes maintained at the expense of rationality and fairness. A public official who erred in the expenditure of public funds could be suspended by the Contraloría and asked to replace misapplied monies. If there were any criminal, as opposed to administrative, wrongdoing, the functionary could be prosecuted in the courts by the Contraloría.

The president, with the unanimous concurrence of his cabinet, could insist on implementing any decree declared illegal by the Contraloría (decree of insistence), except in matters of public expenditures. But this was done only very rarely as it left cabinet members open to possible congressional accusations which could result in removal from office. In a society with numerous and complex laws and sharp ideological divisions, an agency such as the Contraloría had evolved as an interpreter of existing legislation as well as a "guarantor" of legalism.[31]

Perhaps even more important for the purposes of the argument at hand than the autonomy of the other "coequal" branches of government was the marked autonomy of many agencies and organizations within the executive branch itself.[32] What was striking about the Chilean bureaucracy was not how much power it gave the chief executive but how difficult it was for him to control its day-to-day activities. This was so because most public institutions lay outside the executive chain of command in the "decentralized agencies." Such entities determined much of their own budgets and controlled their own hiring practices even though they were nominally controlled by one of the fourteen government ministries. Forty percent of all public employees in Chile worked for the more than fifty semiautonomous bureaus. They generally provided the bulk of economic and social services in areas such as agriculture, housing, social security, and economic development. While they willingly accepted any efforts by the administration to increase their jurisdiction and functions, they strongly resisted attempts to decrease them or to change in any dramatic way the nature of programming and the style of action. Many of the Christian Democrats' innovative programs in housing and urban development were thwarted by the unwillingness of semiautonomous agencies to follow changed guidelines for programming and investments.[33]

By law a president could not remove civil servants in order to replace them with a new cadre more congenial to his policy objectives. New presidents were thus forced to create new agencies to carry out their programs. Often a new agency would duplicate the tasks of an older one, further complicating the problem of coordination and intensifying the competition for a share of the limited governmental budget.[34]

Another characteristic of Chilean institutions which simultaneously reinforced this autonomy and contributed to the "institutionalization" of decision-making was the formal inclusion of private interests in state boards and agencies. The result was that key areas of the economy were dominated by essentially "private" governments. The boards of many government agencies included one-third representation from private interests, one-third from technical experts, and one-third from the government. According to one study, during the period 1958–64 the four most powerful business organizations had voting membership in all the major financial and policy institutions, including the Central Bank, the State Bank, and CORFO.[35] Each business group had voting power on the government bureaus relevant to their particular economic sector. Before the Agrarian Reform Law was passed in 1966, it was difficult to carry out any initiatives in rural reform because 30 percent of the vote in the key agencies was controlled by economic interests that would be adversely affected by reforms.[36] The Frei government moved to give more effective representation in these state agencies to organizations of the middle and working classes.

The intermingling of private and public in the state sector was also reinforced by the existence of strong professional associations and union organizations. In several important cases, professional groups had become influential in governmental agencies. Architects, for example, dominated the Ministry of Housing. The Ministry of Public Works was the almost exclusive fiefdom of civil engineers, and the Ministry of Agriculture was staffed by agronomists and a few veterinarians. A university degree in a particular field was sometimes a prerequisite for appointment or advancement in a given agency, thus guaranteeing privileged employment opportunities for a small group of individuals. The professional standards and outlooks of a particular association, in addition to its vested interests, contributed to the formation of public policy that was often quite different from that being advocated by the political executive and his allies.[37]

But the other countries in Latin America had also seen the rise of strong state institutions and a fragmented policy-making process without a lessening of praetorian political tendencies. The key to the Chilean system, which differentiated it sharply from that in countries like Argentina, was the continuing importance of political party networks and the existence of viable arenas of accommodation, notably the Parliament.[38] At first glance the parties seem to have been merely another layer of organization in the complex Chilean political pluralism. In fact, the party structures which permeated all levels of society were the crucial linkage mechanism binding organizations, institutions, groups, and individuals to the political center. Local units of all parties were active within each level of the bureaucracy, each labor union, each student federation, and each professional association. Parties often succeeded in capturing a particular organization or in setting up a rival one. Once an issue affecting the organization or group arose, the party structures were instrumental in conveying the demands of the organization or group to the nucleus of the policy-making process, where the legislature played a fundamental role.

The Chilean Congress, as early as the 1850s, began to establish a tradition of independence from the executive when it delayed approval of the presidential budget in exchange for concessions on other legislative matters.[39] Though it lost its position as the preeminent institution, which it had enjoyed for thirty years around the turn of the century, by mid-century it still was one of the strongest legislative bodies in the world. The Congress retained final authority over the approval of laws. It could create new programs, abolish old ones, and reduce or modify budgets. The legislature was instrumental in the creation of the complex and unwieldy social security system, and until the constitutional reforms of 1970 it was the key arena for negotiation on the all-important question of salary readjustment. The Senate could even block the president from traveling abroad, as it did during the Frei administration. Congressional committees not only played important roles in the drafting of legislation but served as investigatory bodies. It was in the halls of Congress or through the good offices of deputies or senators from all parties that key compromises were structured between the executive and the opposition on major policy matters such as agrarian reform and copper nationalization. And even more significantly for the stability of the system, it was in the legislature that disparate party factions reached compromises on less important issues of mutual benefit to constituents.

While the conciliation and compromise which took place in the chambers and meeting rooms of the Chilean Congress can be attributed in part to socialization of "institutional norms," shared norms were far less important in explaining the functioning of the system than were other factors. The continuing relevance of the legislature as an arena of compromise was due to the fact that no party or coalition was capable of displacing another. There simply were no giants in the system, and it was clearly to the benefit of all to work within the ongoing mechanisms rather than attempt to destroy them. This was the case because in the final analysis electoral success was the most important measure of a party's power. Additionally, each party and coalition required concrete benefits for supporters in order to maximize their electoral fortunes. The deadlock of political forces was thus accompanied by a strong need to process a whole array of favors for individuals and groups through party networks. The pragmatism of some of the parties of the Center facilitated this process, but all parties had congressional specialists dealing in the mundane side of politics. As noted earlier, benefits were obtained not only through logrolling in the legislature but through direct appeals by individual legislators capable of approaching a bureaucracy sensitive to the influence of the Parliament and its leaders over budget allotments and staff positions. The overwhelming majority of legislators were convinced that they had to pay significant attention to this "casework" in order to ensure their own political careers and the viability of the electoral support of their parties.[40]

The fundamental issue around which much of the politics of conciliation revolved was the attainment by groups and individuals of their *reivindicaciones*, or just demands.[41] For the most part these involved wage readjustments, which are critical in an economy plagued by a high rate of inflation. Table 5 shows the annual variation of the consumer price index from 1952 to 1970. During the first three years of the decade inflation was relatively low, but it reached 46 percent in 1964 and averaged 25.7 percent over the ten-year period.[42] At the same time, Chile experienced a generally slow economic growth rate, with the per capita growth of the national product amounting to an estimated 1.6 percent from 1915 to 1964, though the industrial growth rate was 4.3 percent in the same period.[43] The latter index rose 7 percent in the early 1960s, only to decline to an average of 2.4 percent from 1967 to 1970. The distribution of income also remained sharply skewed, with 60 percent of the population commanding 28 percent of the national income and 14 percent commanding 42 percent. Indeed, the top 2 percent of the Chilean population enjoyed 12.5 percent of the nation's income. Consequently, the main preoccupation of labor unions and other private and public groups was the attainment of income readjustments commensurate with or possibly above the estimated increase in the cost of living. Inflation, therefore, set the basic parameters for the bargaining system. Since the government and its agencies regulated both salary and price increases, the battle over *reajustes* was fought in the public arena and the principal compromises were hammered out in the legislature.

Given the intensity of party polarization in Chile, it is quite likely that an institution like the Congress could not have been created in the mid-twentieth century. But the legislature as an arena of accommodation and as the principal focus of party politics had emerged before the polarization of the party system. It also predated the development of strong state institutions and a centralized bureaucracy.

This had a profound effect on future development. It meant that even with the development of bureaucratic agencies designed to foster economic development and redistribute wealth, political parties with legislative linkages continued to be the principal political networks of the system. Though legislators would increasingly be limited in their ability to generate resources in the Congress itself, they would continue to be the key brokers between constituents and the bureaucracy. By implication, this reinforced the viability of representative institutions. Where a strong bureaucracy emerged before a strong party system, as in Brazil and Argentina, the prospect for the development of informal or officially sponsored linkage networks without popular representation was much greater. Under such circumstances, the chances of maintaining or fostering democratic institutions was severely undermined.[44]

Table 5. Yearly Rates of Inflation, 1952 to 1970 (in percentages)

	Consumer Price Index, Retail		Consumer Price Index, Wholesale	
Year	Variation from December-December	Yearly Average Variation	Variation from December-December	Yearly Average Variation
1952	12.1	22.2	20.9	24.0
1953	56.1	25.3	35.2	23.0
1954	71.1	72.2	65.3	56.9
1955	83.8	75.1	82.8	76.3
1956	37.7	56.1	45.9	63.1
1957	17.3	26.8	34.5	43.2
1958	32.5	25.9	25.3	25.5
1959	33.3	38.6	25.2	30.0
1960	5.4	11.6	1.6	5.3
1961	9.7	7.7	1.6	0.8
1962	27.7	13.9	26.8	8.3
1963	45.4	44.3	45.4	53.7
1964	38.4	46.0	43.7	50.6
1965	25.9	28.8	24.5	24.4
1966	17.0	22.9	19.7	22.9
1967	21.9	18.1	19.8	19.3
1968	27.9	26.6	33.1	30.5
1969	29.3	30.6	39.4	36.5
1970	34.9	32.5	33.7	36.1

SOURCE: Data from Dirección de Estadística y Censos, found in Ricardo Ffrench-Davis, *Políticas económicas en Chile, 1952–1970* (Santiago: Ediciones Nueva Universidad, 1973), pp. 242–46. Ffrench-Davis has made some minor corrections in these figures. The official figures are being used for comparison purposes with the figures of the Allende years.

The existence of a viable legislature with a long tradition, the continuing polarization and competitiveness of Chilean politics, and the need to accommodate particularistic demands contributed to the perpetuation of a politics of accommodation and compromise. The polarization and competitiveness of Chilean party politics made accommodation necessary. The "clientelism" of electoral politics made it possible.

It was inevitable that in such a system of accommodation, change could only be incremental. Depending on the coalition, and the position of the centrist party of the moment, policies would be either reformist or oriented toward the status quo. Constant demands for particular rewards with the availability of resources for only a small number of new programs made it almost impossible to find adequate funding for long-range projects or dramatic new initiatives. A disparity existed in Chile between calls for structural change and transformation and the realities of an incrementalist bargaining system.[45] This disparity problably contributed to the pervasive feeling of permanent crisis in Chilean politics. And yet, because of the acceptance of votes as the key political currency of the system, the necessity of bargaining in a highly competitive, though polarized, atmosphere, and the weight of incrementalist decision-making itself, Chilean elites had been able in the past to conciliate their differences when serious confrontations seemed imminent.

Chilean Politics and the Chilean Military

In the comings and goings of Chilean politics, the armed forces were at the periphery of the political process. Not since the period 1924–31 had they actively intervened to determine the fate of governments. Even then, the armed forces ruled directly for a very short period of time. The administration of General Ibañez from 1927 to 1931 was an elected government which relied on the tacit rather than the active support of the military. It was based more on the political figure of the leader than on the organized participation of the institution in the governing process.[46]

For the most part the officer corps interacted little with the leadership of social, economic, and political institutions.[47] Though respected as professional soldiers and as bearers of a glorious military tradition, they were generally looked down upon by other elites, who considered them narrow and uneducated.[48] That does not mean, however, that the military did not have influence over important policy areas, particularly those dealing with military affairs. Historically, the military has fared well in Chile. In recent years Chile ranked sixth in Latin America in per capita military expenditures and fifth in the size of the armed forces relative to the size of the population.[49]

A tradition of nonintervention in political affairs, however, should not be taken as proof that the Chilean military was above conspiratorial politics. In fact, in practically every administration since the 1930s there have been military incidents which revealed that sectors within the officer corps would have been happy to throw the politicians out. As recently as the mid-fifties a strong movement (the *Linea Recta*) developed in the army to obtain direct military rule with the support of President Ibañez.[50] Historically, there has been continuous tension between the so-called *golpista* elements, who desire direct intervention, and "constitutionalists," who support the "neutrality" of the armed forces.

During the administrations of Jorge Alessandri and Eduardo Frei, civil-military relations deteriorated significantly. Military expenditures as a percentage of the national budget declined sharply from over 15 percent to an average of 9.8 percent in the Alessandri years and an average of 5.3 percent in the Frei years.[51] Open dissatisfaction with the government's "neglect" of the armed forces led to the resignation of the commander in chief of the navy in 1967. And on 21 October 1969 General Roberto Viaux moved troops from his Tacna regiment on the presidential palace, the first such act of direct military insubordination in decades. Though the movement was quickly put down, it clearly reflected the state of discontent within the military. Viaux, the commander in chief of the navy, and the head of the Santiago garrison of the army would later play important roles in a coup attempt staged shortly after Allende's election to prevent the Popular Unity government from taking office.[52]

For the most part, military officers in Chile probably shared the views of the former commander in chief of the Chilean army who noted that

not only the army, I guarantee, but all of the armed forces have a clear doctrine: military power is consciously subordinated to the political power, the Constitution and the laws. . . . Never could we intervene on our own, because we are disciplined. Furthermore, history demonstrates to us that never has that intervention been necessary, because our governors have a common sense and good judgment.[53]

The final remark is extremely instructive. Nonintervention was conditional on the performance of civilian elites, not on a clear principle of allegiance to civilian rule. Chilean military officers saw themselves as guardians of the constitution. In a survey conducted in 1967 among retired generals, 84 percent agreed (64 percent strongly) that the "military is necessary for the country even if there is no war in order to act as a guardian of the constitution in case a government tries to violate it." Only 16 percent of the officers interviewed disagreed with the statement.[54]

2.

The Late 1960s and the Election of Allende: Socioeconomic Change and Political Crisis

As Juan Linz has noted, the literature on the requisites for stable democracy and the causes of breakdown of democratic regimes has focused on underlying socioeconomic problems as the key independent variables. Without denying the importance of socioeconomic or structural factors, Linz has cautioned against this simple sociological determinism, which views politics as static and neglects to consider variables like leadership or to analyze the dynamics of the political process in explaining complex phenomena such as political breakdowns. Linz holds that the "structural characteristics of societies, the actual and latent conflicts, constitute a series of opportunities and constraints for the social and political actors, men and institutions, which can lead to one or another outcome. We shall start from the assumption that those actors have certain choices that can increase or lower the probability of the persistence and stability of a regime."[1]

This study has already described some of the principal structural characteristics of the Chilean political system at mid-century. It has noted the extent of party competitiveness and polarization, with its tendency to erode a working Center. It has highlighted the differentiation and autonomy of the institutional sector and described the accommodationist politics which resulted from political deadlock and the need to redistribute to diverse social forces the finite resources of a relatively poor society. In doing so, it stressed the precariousness of a political process in a situation where high levels of inflation had resulted from group demands which taxed the economic capabilities of the system. But Chile had survived for decades with such a system and had turned accommodationist politics into a fine art. Is it possible that a severe socioeconomic crisis had finally overwhelmed Chilean politics? Keeping in mind Juan Linz's warning, we cannot proceed without evaluating the socioeconomic dimensions of Chilean society in the period immediately preceding the election of Salvador Allende.

The literature suggests that at least two seemingly contradictory dimensions of economic change should be kept in mind in evaluating potential economic strains. In the first place, a marked decline in the economy, especially one following a period of significant improvement in standards of living, could contribute to a degree of societal frustration capable of undermining political authority.[2] Conversely, the second perspective argues that a sharp improvement in economic development could also disrupt political order. By undermining traditional social relations and encouraging new forms of mobilization, rapid economic change places demands on political institutions which exceed their capacity to respond.[3]

In examining the evidence for the Chilean case it will not be possible to present definitive conclusions about the impact of economic change on the political process. The theoretical literature in question has drawn primarily on retrospective analysis and provides no precise indication as to which of the many possible variables available are most important. Nor does it possess clear criteria on how much change must take place in the value of different indicators to reach the threshold of political breakdown. For this reason, much of the literature is tautological. Socioeconomic factors can be shown to be intense enough to cause a crisis only when a crisis has in fact occurred. Such a formulation leaves open the real possibility that other variables not considered in the analysis contributed to the final denouement.[4]

A resolution of these methodological and theoretical difficulties will of necessity entail further synchronic, and particularly diachronic, cross-national research. That does not mean, however, that in a case study such as this one we cannot come to a good judgment about the relative importance of economic versus political variables. By using time-series data we can evaluate whether changes in the values of certain indicators were greater in the period preceding the breakdown of regime than in previous periods not followed by political breakdown.

The Economic Evidence

An examination of a series of economic indicators for the six-year period preceding the election of Salvador Allende gives little indication of either serious economic decline or of explosive economic growth, with its disruptive potential. It is true that there was a mild recession in 1967, followed by slower rates of growth during the next two years than in the inaugural years of the Christian Democratic administration. However, what is striking about the Chilean data is how positive the Christian Democratic years were in relationship to previous years. As table 6 shows, there was in fact a secular decline in per capita GNP from 1953 to 1959, and it was not until 1963 that the per capita index surpassed that of 1953. Not only was the decline reversed in 1960, but the increase in per capita GNP was clearly better during the course of the Frei administration (1965–70) than it had been during the Alessandri

Table 6. Selected Economic Indices for the Period 1952–1970 (1969 = 100)

Year	Per Capita GNP	Government General Expenditures	Government Investment Expenditures	Government Revenues, Mining Excluded	Government Revenues From Mining	Percentage Readjustment of Real Minimum Wage with Respect to Previous Year	Readjustment of Real Wages and Salaries with Respect to Previous Year	Balance of Payments in 1969 Dollars
1952	79.7	43.0	32.9	30.2	42.8	—	—	−21.5
1953	82.7	48.4	24.8	32.5	25.6	−0.1	—	−27.4
1954	80.8	45.4	25.8	30.7	35.9	−2.1	—	−19.3
1955	80.9	48.3	28.9	32.0	44.2	−10.9	—	0.4
1956	79.8	44.6	29.6	31.4	59.0	−11.1	—	−54.4
1957	78.5	47.9	25.4	35.1	41.6	−4.0	—	−34.2
1958	78.4	45.6	28.5	36.9	27.9	−4.9	—	32.4
1959	77.7	46.4	38.0	38.4	43.6	1.0	—	35.8
1960	78.5	55.9	46.6	45.4	42.0	−6.6	—	−52.2
1961	81.1	60.8	49.2	52.5	33.7	20.9	11.8	−138.7
1962	83.5	69.7	60.2	55.0	45.4	5.5	3.6	−54.7
1963	84.5	61.5	62.4	52.3	45.3	−16.5	−8.7	15.1
1964	86.4	61.6	59.9	52.2	46.7	−2.6	−5.3	63.1
1965	89.6	73.3	84.5	66.4	57.2	7.2	13.9	81.3
1966	96.4	82.8	100.4	77.3	91.4	1.3	10.8	94.3
1967	95.5	88.1	89.3	86.2	87.5	−2.8	13.5	−31.6
1968	96.7	94.6	97.6	93.6	84.2	−4.9	−2.0	109.7
1969	100.0	100.0	100.0	100.0	100.0	−5.2	4.3	80.7
1970	101.4	121.2	102.6	111.4	123.5	−4.5	8.5	—

SOURCE: Ricardo Ffrench-Davis, *Políticas económicas en Chile, 1952–1970* (Santiago: Ediciones Nueva Universidad, 1973), tables 35, 51, 68, and 75.

administration (1959–64); the year 1970 ended in a historic high. Though the minimum wage suffered a decline in the last few years of the Frei administration, overall real wages increased substantially during the same years. A glance back at table 5, which depicts the rate of inflation from 1952 to 1970, presents a similar picture. Though inflation remained high during the Christian Democratic administration, in no year did it reach the high of 45.4 percent experienced in the Alessandri administration or the 83.8 percent rate of the Ibañez administration. Finally, the relatively better economic situation of the late 1960s was accompanied by a positive balance of trade, again a situation with no parallel during the previous two decades.

Table 6 goes beyond merely presenting data on the economy; it also provides information about governmental performance and capability. Not only was the economy in relatively better shape during the Frei years but both government revenues and government expenditures increased dramatically, affording an opportunity for the state to provide a level of services as well as capital and investment improvements unmatched in previous administrations. In real terms, expenditures on health, housing, and education increased 136 percent, 130 percent, and 167 percent, respectively.[5] Nor was investment shortchanged, as both public and private investment grew significantly.

By all indications, then, the period immediately preceding the advent to power of the *Unidad Popular* (or U.P.) was not characterized by a mounting and unprecedented secular crisis in the Chilean economy. The mid-fifties were far worse in every respect from an economic point of view. And during that period, governmental capabilities, measured in terms of taxation and expenditures, also experienced decline or stagnation. Nor is there any indication that economic transformations in the late 1960s were too dramatic or strong. Increases in standards of living were modest, but better than before, and government capability, measured strictly in terms of available resources, clearly stayed ahead.

Under such conditions, one would have to say that social mobilization resulting directly from economic deprivation, relative deprivation, or economically induced social dislocation would have been less in the 1960s than in previous years. Paradoxically, many observers have noted that in fact social and political mobilization increased substantially during the late 1960s. What were the dimensions of that mobilization? If it was massive, how did it come about, given the analysis of the economic situation? Could social and political mobilization, developing independent of a severe economic crisis, have had a destabilizing impact on the system?

Political and Social Mobilization in the Late 1960s

Observers of Latin American politics have noted that in the early 1960s Chile may have ranked first in democratic stability in Latin America, but it ranked fourteenth in electoral participation.[6] As figure 1 shows, voter partici-

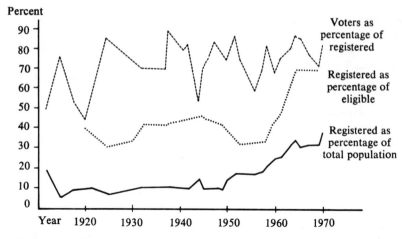

Figure 1. Political Participation, 1912–70

Source: Electoral data from the Dirección General del Registro Electoral, Santiago, Chile. Demographic information from Dirección de Estadística y Censos, "Población total por provincias de Chile, 1885–60" (Santiago, 1964); idem, "Población del pais" (Santiago, 1964); and *El Mercurio*, 4 September 1970, pp. 11, 12.

pation was restricted during the parliamentary republic in the early part of the century, so that it was not until the 1950s, with the adoption of female suffrage, that the electoral participation rate exceeded that of 1912. This reduced voter participation was primarily the result of electoral laws which restricted voting to the literate population and made it necessary to register periodically in order to stay on the electoral rolls. Low mobilization was reinforced by the fact that Marxist parties did not turn to the countryside to seek electoral bases. In fact, rural unionization was illegal until 1967. Marxist parties concentrated on gaining support among the growing industrial proletariat. Reduced participation was also reinforced by the clientelistic electoral system favored by both the Right and the Center, which in turn undermined populist appeals until the rise of Carlos Ibañez in the 1950s. Underlying this state of affairs was a tacit agreement between rural and urban elites. Rural elites were willing to endure the hardship of price controls on agricultural goods imposed by an industrially oriented middle class which relied, during the Radical years, on support from the parties of the Left with similar interests. In turn, centrist and leftist parties did not alter the basic political and social structure of the landed elite.[7]

An important turning point in electoral mobilization came with the electoral reforms of 1958 and 1962. These reforms not only did away with periodical registries but also established rules requiring voter registration and mechanisms to enforce those rules. Thus a citizen who failed to register and vote could be punished by a prison term. Even more significantly, since prison terms were rarely imposed, government agencies and banks were required to ask for the electoral registration certificate to process any service.[8] These requirements, and the increased activities of the parties, meant that the electorate expanded from 1.25 million, or 16 percent of the population, in 1960, to 2.84 million, or 28.3 percent of the population, in 1971.[9]

Dramatic as these increases in voter turnout are, it must be cautioned that voter participation is perhaps not the best indicator of destabilizing mobilization. Quite to the contrary, voting is not a very demanding act, and increased turnout can be taken as an indicator of increased participation within the framework of the ongoing system. It is necessary to turn to other indicators of mobilization to better evaluate the extent of social demands on the Chilean system in the late 1960s.

Henry Landsberger and Tim McDaniel have argued that "uncontrolled" mobilization or "hypermobilization" began in Chile "not in 1970, but in 1965, by the assumption to power of the PDC. A flood was released and further stimulated, as manifested by rising union membership and a rising rate of strike activity. This flood did not lead on to 'fortune,' because it could not even be rechanneled, let alone contained...."[10] Unionization and strike activity clearly are better indicators of "uncontrolled" mobilization than is electoral turnout. Our task will be to analyze the evidence on the extent of mobilization and attempt to evaluate the character of that mobilization.

Table 7 presents information on the growth of industrial and craft unions from 1937 to 1970. It is immediately apparent that during the Frei period the absolute rate of growth for these unions was substantial. Industrial unions grew by 38 percent and craft unions grew by 90 percent. At first glance it would appear that this was an unprecedented development in Chilean history, signaling a dramatic change in the mobilization of the urban working class. More detailed examination, however, reveals that the upward trend in the 1960s was primarily a period of recuperation from a decline in union membership both in real and relative terms during the 1950s. What is striking about the information presented in the table is that despite the increased level of unionization in the Christian Democratic administration, the percentage of the industrial population organized in industrial unions was still lower in 1970 (35.1 percent) than it had been in 1953 (38.3 percent). And despite the dramatic increase in craft union membership in the late 1960s, the percentage of organized workers in the nonagricultural sector rose from only 19.3 percent in 1953 to 19.4 percent in 1970. The union population kept pace with general changes in society, but did not exceed those changes in any dramatic way. This can be appreciated by surveying the growth of industries eligible for unionization. Between the 1957 and the 1967 industrial censuses the number of industries employing more than twenty workers (an industry was required to have twenty-five to form an industrialized union) rose from 1,875 to 3,468,

Table 7. Growth of Industrial and Craft Unions in Selected Years, 1932 to 1970

Year	Number of Industrial Unions	Number of Members in Industrial Unions	Active Population, Industry	Percentage of Industrial Population Unionized	Number of Craft Unions	Number of Members in Craft Unions	Total Nonagricultural Work Force	Total Nonagricultural Work Force Unionized	Percentage of Work Force Unionized
1932	168	29,442	205,000	14.4	253	25,359	801,000	54,801	0.07
1934	266	42,617			414	38,468		81,085	
1936	275	51,185			315	35,514			
1938	333	78,989			599	46,983			
1940	629	91,940	298,100	33.9	1,259	70,357	965,100	180,497	18.7
1942	602	122,688			991	71,641			
1944	596	143,860			1,056	103,221			
1946	591	148,276			1,115	103,498			
1948	607	151,633			1,250	112,043			
1950	626	147,306			1,270	111,994			
1952	635	155,054	405,100	38.3	1,393	128,329	1,489,700	288,131	19.3
1954	667	165,888			1,372	132,161			
1956	788	170,689			1,563	144,303			
1958	641	154,650			1,225	119,666			
1960	608	122,306	406,000	30.1	1,144	107,687	1,605,900	229,981	14.3
1962	598	134,478			1,154	110,669			
1964	632	142,951			1,207	125,926			
1966	990	179,506			1,679	161,363			
1968	1,261	189,815			2,163	222,212			
1970	1,440	197,651	562,900	35.1	2,569	239,323	2,256,200	436,974	19.4

SOURCE: Union data for 1932–58, James O. Morris and Roberto Oyaneder, *Afiliación y finanzas sindicales en Chile* (Santiago: INSORA, 1962), pp. 18–20; for 1960–68, Instituto Nacional de Estadísticas, *Finanzas, bancos, cajas sociales año 1969* (Santiago, The Institute, 1969), p. 153; for 1970, *Mensaje del Presidente Allende ante el Congreso Pleno*, 21 May 1972, pp. 859–61. Census data for 1930, Universidad de Chile, Instituto de Economía, *Desarrollo económico de Chile, 1940–1956* (Santiago: Editorial Universitaria, 1956), table A25. Census data for 1940 and 1952, Dirección de Estadísticas y Censos, *Cifras comparativas de los censos de 1940 y 1952 muestra del censo de 1960* (n.d.) p. 9. Population figures for 1970, ODEPLAN, *Plan de la economía nacional* (1971) p. 62. Population data are provided only for census years.

a rise of 85 percent.[11] During the same period the number of unions rose 83 percent. Since the number of unionized workers in the same period rose 23 percent, the average size of unions declined as more small industries became organized. In 1958 the average union had 248 workers, while in 1967 it had 162.

It must be noted further that the total number of union members has been overstated in table 7. This is so because many of the craft union members are also members of industrial unions. In 1967, for example, about 20 percent of the craft union members were also members of a plant union. Furthermore, it is likely that during the 1960s the proportion of craft union members holding dual membership increased rather than decreased. Legislation was enacted during the Frei government to upgrade the classification of several industrial crafts from *obrero* (blue-collar worker) to *empleado* (white-collar worker), which meant an increase in status and government benefits for those favored. In order to guarantee the new status and benefits, workers would routinely petition to form a craft union. The fact that unionization seemed merely to keep pace with general trends in Chilean society, and that much of the unionization which took place during this period was the result of legislation, detracts considerably from its value as an indicator of "uncontrolled mobilization." In fact it can be argued, as Clotario Blest, the founder of the Chilean labor federation, has done, that the growth of craft unions is an indicator of potential weakening of the labor movement as a militant force rather than of increased strength.[12] The empleado status of many craft unions drives a sharp wedge into the solidarity of the working class by dramatizing social distinctions. Furthermore, craft unions are weak in terms of collective bargaining rights, meaning that empleado status is often sought despite the fact that it might lower the ability of the group in question to carry out trade union functions.[13]

The 1960s, then, saw a resumption of the secular pattern of growth which began with the Popular Front government elected in 1938. The decline of the labor movement in the 1950s was due to economic crisis and the repression of labor by the Ibañez administration. (Ibañez maintained the ban on the Communist party until 1958.) It was also due to the sharp divisions and disarray in the leadership ranks of the movement. The 1960s, and especially the Frei administration, marked not only a period of labor organization but also a period of substantial reform and active government encouragement of the union movement.

Perhaps the most dramatic indicator of the favorable attitude of the government toward reform was its active organization of the heretofore unorganized rural workers. Over two hundred rural unions were organized before the passage of legislation in 1967 allowing the formal establishment of rural unions. As table 8 shows, by November of 1970 136,984 rural workers were unionized, whereas only five years earlier there were a mere 2,118 organized

Table 8. Growth of Agricultural Unions

Year	Number of Unions	Total Number of Members
1925	10	5,000
1953	15	1,042
1958	28	2,030
1960	18	1,424
1961	22	1,831
1962	22	1,860
1963	22	1,500
1964	24	1,658
1965	32	2,118
1966	201	10,417
1967	211	42,474
1968	371	78,419
1969	421	104,666
1970 (through November)	476	136,984

SOURCE: For 1925, Alan Angell, *Politics and the Labour Movement in Chile* (London: Oxford University Press, 1972), p. 37; for 1953, Servicio Nacional de Estadísticas, *Estadística Chilena, Sinopsis 1958;* for 1960–68, Instituto Nacional de Estadísticas, *Finanzas, bancos y cajas sociales año 1969,* (Santiago: The Institute, 1969); p. 153; for 1969–70, Dirección de Presupuestos, *Balance consolidado del sector público de Chile años 1969–1970 y período 1964–1970,* p. 41.

workers in the countryside. This meant that by 1970, 18 percent of the active population in agriculture was organized, an unprecedented organizational effort for such a short period of time. It is here that one finds the best indicator of significant mobilization during the late 1960s prior to the advent of the government of Salvador Allende.[14]

Yet even this mobilization must be kept in perspective. By 1970 organized rural workers represented less than 5 percent of the active population, so that in terms of society as a whole the organizational effort was not great. Furthermore, over 80 percent of the population in the countryside remained unorganized. More importantly, rural unionization was rarely the result of spontaneous, uncontrolled mobilization. It was a deliberate policy, sanctioned by legislation and conducted primarily by government agencies. The fact that toward the end of the period political parties became active in the unionization effort, and that some agencies of the government were less willing to move fast in the countryside than others, does not detract from the main point that the process of rural unionization was a highly organized and controlled one.[15]

Turning to another possible indicator of mobilization, the incidence of strikes by the labor movement, we see that the 1960s and in particular the Christian Democratic administration witnessed a dramatic increase in strike activity (see table 9). Whereas in 1960 the country experienced 245 strikes, in 1966 that number had increased to 1,073. If we compare the penultimate years of the Alessandri and Frei administrations we can see that the incidence of strikes as well as the number of workers affected by strikes went up 135

Table 9. Evolution of Strikes, 1947–69

Year	Number of Unions	Number of Strikes	Average Strike per Union	Number of Strikers	Percentage of Strikers over Active Population	Number of Workers per Strike	Total Man-days Lost in Strikes	Man-days Lost per Strike	Days per Strike per Worker
1947–50	1858	121	.07	44,603		369	1,194,885	9,875	26.8
1952	1982	215	.11	151,715	.10	706	1,766,827	8,218	11.6
1954	2049	305	.15	74,696		246	905,849	2,970	12.1
1956	2351	147	.06	105,438		717	1,657,194	11,273	15.7
1959	1732	204	.12	82,188		403	869,728	4,263	10.6
1960	1752	245	.14	88,518	.06	361	—	—	—
1963	1830	416	.23	117,084		281	—	—	—
1965	2010	723	.39	182,359		259	2,015,253	1,878	10.3
1966	2669	1073	.40	195,435		182	972,382	995	3.5
1969	3749	977	.26	275,406	.12	281			
Percentage change, 1959–69	105	135		135					

SOURCE: For 1947–50, Universidad de Chile, Instituto de Economía, *Desarrollo económico de Chile, 1952–56* (Santiago: Editorial Universitaria, 1956), p. 7; 1952–56. Servicio Nacional de Estadística, *Estadística de Chile Sinopsis 1958* (Santiago: Direccion Nacional de Estadistica y Censos, 1958); 1959–69, *Mensaje Presidencial, 1970.* p. 366.

percent. Increased strike activity closely paralleled the increase in number of unions (105 percent) in the same two years. This suggests that the increase in strike activity was probably stimulated more by the proliferation of new organizations than by the addition of members to old ones. This observation is supported by the evidence that the average number of workers per strike decreased substantially from the 1950s to the 1960s. In the earlier period there were fewer unions to call strikes, but they involved a proportionally larger number of workers in each strike. Likewise, it can be noted that while the average number of strikes called per union shot up in 1965 and 1966, in 1969 it was at a level similar to that of 1963. Finally, column five helps to place the significance of strike activity in perspective. It shows that for the census years of 1952, 1960, and 1970 the proportion of strikers to total active population varied little—from 10 percent to 6 percent to 12 percent, respectively.[16]

But if strike activity is merely a reflection of the increasing number of unions, and, as we noted earlier, the increased number of unions did not lead (except in the rural areas) to substantial new mobilization, relative to growth in the society, how significant is the increased strike activity as an indicator of "uncontrolled" mobilization? Neither the number of strikes nor the number of strikers seems to be an indicator of *massive* change. And yet the size and number of strikes may be less important in judging mobilization than the *intensity* of strike activity. Did strikes become more intense in the late 1960s? Table 9 reports the total man-days lost in strikes, which is an indicator of strike intensity, since it suggests the number of days strikers were willing to stay off the job. In Chile this was a particularly good measure because of the severe lack of adequate strike support funds, which rendered any strike a real hardship for the workers involved. The evidence reported is noteworthy, but it contradicts what might be expected. The absolute number of days lost per year to strikes was substantially higher in *absolute* terms in the early 1950s than in the late 1960s. This was the case despite the fact that the active population in the early 1950s was 50 percent smaller than in the late 1960s. Likewise, the average duration of a strike was considerably higher in 1947–50, when the figure was 26.8 days, than in 1969, when it was 3.5.

What is important about these figures is that strikes were of longer duration and were much more costly both to the country and to the workers in a period when the government was much more likely to repress workers. The short duration of strikes in the Frei administration is a clear indicator of a deliberate government policy aimed at settling labor disputes in the worker's favor. The restrictive and antilabor Labor Code, with its ludicrous definition of what constituted a legal strike and its penalties for so-called illegal strikes, was applied less in favor of the employers and more in favor of the workers. Ironically, it was this same favorable predisposition toward workers, rather than mass alienation, which stimulated the increase in unionization and strikes. With the relaxation of government repression, workers were much freer to take the initiative, secure in the knowledge that their actions would receive favorable government response. As Alan Angell notes, "the sharp increase in strikes since 1965 need not be interpreted as a Marxist attempt to heighten the class war. It was more likely due to the fact that the government was more sympathetic to unions; that the number of unions and unionists increased considerably; that a larger labour inspectorate meant more attempts at conciliation and less use of police repression; and, of course, to national strikes, especially in 1967-68, against national-income policies."[17]

This interpretation of the origins of increased strike activity is similar to the one advanced earlier to explain worker unionization, particularly rural unionization. It was a response to a deliberate policy on the part of the government to include people who had been left behind. It was part of the same strategy which led to "popular promotion" schemes with other disenfranchised elements, namely the urban slum dwellers and urban squatters. Though government figures on the success of the *juntas de vecinos* and *centros de madres* are exaggerated, many new neighborhood organizations sprang up initially under government sponsorship (promoción popular) and later under the sponsorship of rival political parties, primarily on the Left.[18]

The Late 1960s: Political Crisis

The previous analysis helps to explain how participation increased despite the lack of dramatic changes in the economy. Political factors, rather than simple economic ones, were the critical variables in explaining the change in mobilization patterns. After a period of deliberate governmental demobilization, which undermined many of the gains that the working class had achieved during the Popular Front period, the government once again adopted a favorable attitude toward popular involvement in the political economic life of the nation. Both through relaxation of governmental repression and a deliberate policy of popular mobilization, which extended for the first time into the countryside, the Christian Democratic administration was able to match and surpass previous rates of popular mobilization.

Precisely because Chilean mobilization did not tax the economic system, and because it developed in response to deliberate governmental policy, one could advance the proposition that it presented a good example of what Gabriel Almond has called "responsive performance." As Almond notes, "participation in and of itself tends to be a valued activity and may be viewed as a demand. And when a political system legitimates participatory activity on the part of different groups of the population, it may be said to be responding to these demands."[19]

Mobilization was not in itself a threat. It represented increased participation which could easily have been absorbed by the Chilean political system, had not the system experienced an important transformation. But that qualifier is extremely important and is the key to understanding the role of social mobilization in the Chilean crisis. It is a mistake to identify the mobilization of the late 1960s as an example of "responsive performance," not so much because of the nature of mobilization per se, but because of basic changes in Chilean politics, which transformed any kind of mobilization into a potentially destabilizing force. Nor was the gap between mobilization and the ability of the system to cope with mobilization simply a matter of the erosion of key political institutions such as Chile's strong political parties. In fact, during the late 1960s Chilean parties became stronger and more institutionalized than ever before. What changed were the traditional rules of the game and accommodationist politics, revolving around the legislature, that had made it possible for strong political actors and institutions to compromise and to structure a working consensus. According to this interpretation, the political crisis preceded the social mobilization of new groups and the more dangerous countermobilization of established interests. There is no doubt that during the Allende administration both types of mobilization would get out of hand and have seriously destabilizing effects. But initially, mobilization in Chile was less a cause of impending crisis than a symptom of crisis at the center of the political system. And though that crisis came to a head in the Allende years, its roots must be sought earlier, particularly in the Christian Democratic administration of Eduardo Frei.

One of the most important factors contributing to a qualitative change in the nature of the political system was the first appearance of a relatively cohesive centrist movement with an ideological rather than a pragmatic outlook. The largely pragmatic Radicals had been challenged earlier by the surge movement of Carlos Ibañez and the "apolitical" conservatism of Jorge Alessandri. But it was not until the emergence of the Christian Democrats as the new Center in Chilean politics that the Radicals clearly lost ground as a major political force.

. Unlike the fragmented and poorly organized Ibañistas, the Christian Democrats had a talented and cohesive leadership group with the resources and energy to try to capture the Center of the political spectrum with an unprecedented organizational effort. Arguing that Christian Democracy provided an alternative to liberal capitalism and Marxist socialism, they consciously sought to break the polarization of Chilean politics by capturing the Center pole and turning it into a new centrist tendency. From 9.4 percent of the vote in the congressional election of 1957 (as the *Falange Nacional*), the Christian Democrats captured 15.4 percent in 1961 and finally overtook the Radicals with 22 percent (to the Radical 20.8 percent) in the municipal elections of 1963. As table 10 shows, the rise of the Christian Democrats paralleled the slower but steady rise of the Left. It is important to note that the success of the Christian Democrats was not gained at the expense of the Radicals, but rather

ble 10. Percentage of the Vote Received by Major Chilean Parties, 1937–73

Political Preference	1937	1941	1945	1949	1953	1957	1961	1965	1969	1973
ht										
Conservatives	21.3	17.2	23.6	22.7	14.4	17.6	14.3	5.2	—	—
Liberals	20.7	14.0	20.1	19.3	10.9	15.4	16.1	7.3	—	—
Nationals	—	—	—	—	—	—	—	—	20.0	21.3
nter										
Radicals	18.7	23.0	19.9	27.7	15.6	22.1	21.4	13.3	13.0	3.7
Christian Democrats or Falangists	—	3.4	2.6	3.9	2.9	9.4	15.4	42.3	29.8	29.1
Democrats	9.4	5.7	5.4	6.8	5.6	5.0	6.9	—	—	—
Agrarian Laborists (Ibañista)	—	—	—	8.3	18.9	7.8	—	—	—	—
ft										
Socialists	11.2	22.1	12.8	9.4	14.2	10.7	10.7	10.3	12.2	18.7
Communists	4.2	11.8	10.3	—	—	—	11.4	12.4	15.9	16.2
her	14.5	2.8	5.3	1.9	17.5	12.0	3.8	9.2	9.1	11.0
tal	100.0	100.0	100.0	100.0	100.0	100.0	100.0	100.0	100.0	100.0

SOURCE: Calculated from data available in the Dirección del Registro Electoral, Santiago, Chile.

at the expense of the Conservative and Liberal parties and fragments of the Ibañista movement. Support for the rightist party declined from 29.2 percent of the vote in 1957 to 23.6 percent in 1963.

The new strength of the Christian Democrats put them in a very good position for the 1964 presidential election. When each of the major parties had presented candidates in 1958, Allende, representing the Communist and Socialist alliance, had lost the election by 33,416 votes (of 1,235,552 cast). When a candidate presented by the alliance of Radicals, Liberals, and Conservatives lost a crucial by-election to the Left in the months before the 1964 presidential contest, the Liberals and Conservatives threw their support to Eduardo Frei, the Christian Democratic candidate. He proceeded to win the election by a comfortable margin of 56.1 percent of the vote to 38.9 percent for Salvador Allende, the candidate of a united Left.[20]

The Christian Democrats in Chile were not the only ones interested in a third alternative for Chile. The Kennedy administration's Alliance for Progress called for changes that would benefit new industrial groups to the detriment of the more traditional elites with ties to the land. Significant reforms would help to undermine the potential for another Cuba in Latin America. The Christian Democrats in Chile were the logical group to receive strong support for a preemptive effort to undermine the threat of the Left while bringing about a measure of development. The 1964 election saw an unprecedented interference in Chilean politics from external sources. The Central Intelligence Agency channeled three million dollars to the Frei campaign, which also received substantial sums of money from European and private business sources. The CIA also undertook to support the Frei effort by mounting a massive propaganda campaign. The campaign, referred to in Chile as a "campaign of terror," sought to depict the Allende candidacy as one that would institute a repressive and bloody regime in which, among other things, children would be taken away from their mothers. There is little doubt that that vituperative propaganda campaign contributed to the sharp rise in conflict and mistrust in Chilean politics.[21]

Once in office the Christian Democrats moved ahead vigorously to implement their program. They made it clear from the outset that a major component of the program would be the incorporation into the nation's political life of sectors that had previously been excluded. With overt and covert support from the United States, they embarked on a massive effort to organize what were referred to as "marginal" segments of society.[22] All other political forces in the country, ranging from Conservatives to Communists, were put on the defensive as the Christian Democrats made it clear that they intended to break the deadlock of electoral strength by capturing the allegiance of a majority of the population. Indeed Frei's victory had suggested that the party already had an unprecedented degree of majority support. From the outset the Radicals came in for harsh criticism.[23] Christian Democrats soon moved to challenge that party's hold over much of the bureaucracy. Radicals were accused of being the party of expediency and compromise and of responsibility for the decay of institutions and the lack of progress in meeting the social crisis. The Center had been taken over by a party which openly disdained the political maneuvering of clientelistic politics that for so long had kept the system going. What is even more important, however, is that the Center was able to win not only the presidency but majority support in one chamber of the Congress. In the 1965 congressional elections, for the first time in memory, a single party captured a majority of the Chamber of Deputies with an impressive 42.3 percent of the vote. From that position of strength, exerting considerable discipline over its legislators, the Christian Democrats proceeded to rule as a "single party" (partido único). On major issues such as agrarian reform or copper nationalization, compromises were struck with opposing forces.[24] However, on much of the day-to-day running of the government, with the support of its majority in the Chamber, the government was able to undermine significantly the politics of clientelism.[25] Item vetoes of the executive, upheld in the Chamber of Deputies, cut back on congressional ability to logroll public works bills and to influence salary readjustments. Arguing against the incrementalism which had impeded reform, government technocrats sought to institute more "rational" planning schemes which would dispense with the "distortions" of the political process. Opposition parties and legislators were progressively excluded from many of the particularistic deals of the past. Congress lost some of its earlier importance as an arena of accommodation. The Senate, "refuge" of the opposition, became a largely negative force, going so far as to take the unprecedented step, noted in chapter 1, of barring President Frei from visiting the United States.

The plebiscitarian policies of President Frei would culminate, at the end of his term, in the adoption of constitutional reforms specifically aimed at curbing the role of Congress within the system. The legislature's jurisdiction over budgetary and salary readjustments, in particular, was strongly reduced. Ironically, in light of future developments, the Left, which had always drawn strength from its position in the legislature, voted against most of the reforms. The Right, convinced that former-president Alessandri would be an easy winner in the 1970 race, voted for the reforms.[26] Both the Christian Democrats and the Right would thus inherit a Congress which could serve either as a rubber stamp or a negative force. Even before the election of Allende the institutional mechanisms for accommodation had become weaker and more rigid.

The mobilization of the late 1960s must be understood in light of this *"partido único"* strategy of the Christian Democrats. Their efforts at mobilization and their disdain for some of the traditional clientelistic mechanisms encouraged as never before a frantic race among all sectors to prevent the centrist party from obtaining majority support. The Left moved quickly, if belatedly, into the countryside and *poblaciones* to accelerate its effort to broaden its base among the working class. The Conservatives and Liberals responded to their disastrous 12.5 percent of the vote in the 1965 race by fusing into a National party and turning to the magic name of Alessandri to curb the party which was expropriating their lands and robbing them of electoral strength. While the mobilization per se did not exceed the capabilities of the system, the goal of the mobilization was not only to incorporate new sectors into the political process but to ensure that this incorporation would lead to partisan advantage.

The problem with the Christian Democrats, and with the country, was that they did not succeed in their goal of depolarizing Chilean politics by establishing a new majority. The support for Frei in 1964 and the impressive showing in the congressional election of 1965 merely illustrated the workings of a polarized system. The Center had succeeded with support from the two sides of the political spectrum (with most of the strength coming from the Right) and not through a fundamental shift in political allegiances in the system. The 1969 congressional election vividly illustrated this problem. The Christian Democratic vote dropped to 29.8 percent of the total. The National party made a strong comeback, obtaining 20 percent of the vote, while the Left continued to make headway. The pragmatic Radicals proved to be the only real casualties, dropping to 13 percent of the vote, their lowest level in this century. The Christian Democrats had attempted to govern as if they had become a new political force with widespread support for its claim of representing a "third" way in Chilean politics. But this conviction proved to be an illusion. In fact the Christian Democrats never succeeded in becoming a genuinely new orientation in Chilean politics—a viable centrist tendency capable of eroding the strength of both Right and Left. In Sartori's terms, they continued to represent an unstable pole in the center of the political spectrum. As a convenient option, their support had come about more through a "sum of exclusions," primarily from the Right. With the rapid defection of voters from the Right, and the failure to pick up voters from the Left, the party's strength withered quickly. In the process, the *partido único* stand alienated other political groups and heightened political tensions. The Christian Democrats temporarily broke the deadlock of Chilean politics but failed to restructure the polarized system which had created the deadlock in the first place. By undermining, however unintentionally, the fragile understanding of Chilean politics without altering the traditional correlation of forces they simply aggravated polarization and worsened the deadlock. It is no wonder that it would prove impossible to structure a Center-Right or Center-Left coalition in the coming presidential race of 1970—thus opening the way for a three-way race in which the Right or the Left could win without support from the Center.

This study has stressed the role of the Christian Democrats because of the important role which a strongly ideological Center plays in undermining the fragile consensus of a polarized democratic system. However, that should not be taken to mean that other factors were unimportant even if not decisive. In particular, it is important to stress that the technocratic Christian Democrats were not the only group to question the implications of the old bargaining system. The Left in Chile, during the same period, began to feel a direct challenge from numerically small but increasingly vocal groups who rejected the system of party politics and called for revolutionary transformations through violent means. They drew their inspiration from the Cuban revolution, the Uruguyan Tupamaros, and the struggle of Vietnamese revolutionaries who caught the imagination of students and others in their guerrilla war against the most powerful nation on earth. The most important of these groups was the *Movimiento de Izquierda Revolucionaria* (Revolutionary Left Movement—MIR) founded by students at the University of Concepción.[27] By the late 1960s organizational efforts in the countryside and in working-class neighborhoods began to produce modest results.

The challenge from the Center and the far Left and the adoption of a more revolutionary line within the Socialist, Communist, and even Radical parties, particularly their youth sectors, inevitably heightened the militancy of leftist organizations. The traditional "bourgeois" bargaining system had not only lost much legitimacy but was also less acceptable as a mechanism for ensuring gains—albeit partial ones. The reduction of the effectiveness of those mechanisms would further reinforce such a conclusion. Although erosion of support for the traditional system from the Right would become more visible after the 1970 election, the October 1969 military move by General Viaux had also demonstrated that powerful sectors were tired of the comings and goings of democracy, despite the fact that Jorge Alessandri was widely viewed as the certain winner of the 1970 election. In this atmosphere of heightened competition and political crisis, Chileans prepared for the 1970 presidential contest.

The 1970 Election: The Problem of a Minority President

The election of Salvador Allende to the presidency of Chile in 1970 was not the result of a dramatic shift of the Chilean electorate to the Left. The stark reality is that the significant increases in popular participation and electoral registration during the late 1960s were not channeled, in proportionally higher terms, to the parties of the Left. In fact, as table 11 shows, Allende obtained a smaller percentage of the total vote in that election than he had in the previous presidential election. If we assume that leftist voting patterns for 1964–70 were stable, then Allende was supported by only 55,467, or 13.3 percent, of the 416,731 new voters registered between those years. Since the vote for the Christian Democratic candidate declined dramatically between the two elections, it is quite probable that the conservative Alessandri was the principal beneficiary of the newly mobilized vote. Perhaps more than any other statistic, this one reveals that heightened radicalism was not a principal characteristic of Chilean electoral politics in 1970. Instead, Salvador Allende's election was the result of the inability of Chile's polarized political system to structure a winning majority coalition before the election and was further evidence of erosion of traditional mechanisms of political accommodation.

According to coalition theorists, a coalition situation occurs when three or more actors with actual or perceived preferences which are dissimilar coordinate their actions in order to achieve an outcome which is preferable to that which could be achieved by acting alone.[28] In 1964 such a coalition was structured when the rightist conservatives and liberals backed Eduardo Frei after the disastrous showing of a conservative candidate in a local by-election. The Right feared that the united Left would achieve the victory which they had missed by a narrow 33,416-vote margin in 1958. By 1970, however, sentiment had changed and the Right felt it would be better served by going it alone, supporting the candidacy of independent conservative Jorge Alessandri. Though the Christian Democrats as a group were probably closer in ideological distance to the National party as a whole, and the election of a Marxist was still a clear possibility, conservatives felt a strong contempt for the Frei government, both for its reforms in the countryside and its *partido único* stand. Furthermore, the Christian Democratic candidate for president, Radomiro Tomic, openly sought an alliance not with the Right but with the Left, expressing the prevailing feeling that in a three-way race the conserva-

Table 11. Results of the 1958, 1964, and 1970 Presidential Elections in Chile

	1958			1964			1970	
Candidate	Vote	%	Candidate	Vote	%	Candidate	Vote	%
Allende	356,493	28.5	Allende	977,902	38.6	Allende	1,070,334	36.2
Bossay	192,077	15.4	Frei	1,409,012	55.7	Tomic	821,801	27.8
Frei	255,769	20.5	Duran	125,233	5.0	Alessandri	1,031,159	34.9
Alessandri	389,909	31.2						
Zamorano	41,304	3.3						
Blank and void	14,798	1.1	Blank and void	18,550	0.7	Blank and void	31,505	1.1
Total vote	1,250,350	100.0	Total vote	2,530,697	100.0	Total vote	2,954,799	100.0
Total registration	1,497,902		Total registration	2,915,121		Total registration	3,539,747	
Percent of abstentions	16.5		Percent of abstentions	13.2		Percent of abstentions	16.5	

SOURCE: Compiled from materials in the Dirección del Registro Electoral, Santiago, Chile.

tive candidate would win.[29] However, the Left was not about to accept an alliance with the Christian Democrats, particularly when such an alliance would have involved a Christian Democratic standard-bearer. The Left was dissatisfied with the *partido único* stance and the unwillingness of the Christian Democrats to move further in their reforms and was hopeful that it might be able to pull an upset in a race which divided the opposition into two separate candidacies.[30] Counter to some of the assumptions made in coalition theory, each of the major actors in Chilean politics sought to maximize its position, after a complex set of internal struggles, following the dictates of ideology and its perceptions of past as well as future political events. They were not responding to a narrow set of utilities of a material sort, nor did they have a clear conception of the shifting and contradictory preferences of other actors or a clear vision of what the final outcome would be.[31]

In the three-way contest, the miscalculations of the Right became immediately apparent. Alessandri ran a dismal race and confounded most pollsters by trailing Allende's 36.2 percent of the vote with 34.9 percent—a 39,175-vote difference.[32] What had almost happened in 1958, when centrist parties also ran their own candidates, finally took place in 1970. For the first time in Chilean history, a candidate of the Left, not one merely supported by the Left, had won the highest office in the land.

The results of the race clearly illustrate that the Christian Democrats had been primarily a Center artificially created by the polarization of the system. With the support of the Right, Frei had gained 55.7 percent of the vote in 1964. In 1970, Tomic obtained a mere 27.8 percent of all ballots cast. Table 12 shows the importance of erosion of rightist support for the Christian Democrats over the previous six years. The simple correlation coefficient between the vote for Frei in 1964 and Alessandri in 1970 is actually higher than the correlation between the vote for Frei and Tomic. At the same time the correlation between the vote for Alessandri in 1970 and the Christian Democratic vote in the congressional elections of 1965 and 1969 declined sharply while the correlation between the 1970 vote for Tomic and Christian Democratic support in those elections increased.

The basic fact of the Allende presidency from the very outset was that it constituted a minority presidency. Though Tomic's platform was similar in many ways to Allende's, it would be a serious mistake to argue that Allende's program for dramatic social change received the backing of a majority of the population.[33] The combined votes that Tomic and Allende received in 1970 amounted to more than 50 percent of the total vote cast. However, aggregate data suggest that Tomic was more likely to draw support from areas where Alessandri was strong than from areas where Allende had electoral strength. The simple correlation between the vote for Tomic and the vote for Alessandri in all Chilean communes was .31. By contrast, the same correlation with the Allende vote was -.64, similar to the correlation of -.77 between Allende and Alessandri. Furthermore, survey data suggest that many Tomic voters, reflect-

Table 12. Simple Correlation Coefficients between the 1970 Votes for Tomic and Alessandri and the Vote for Frei in 1964 and for the Christian Democrats in the 1965 and 1969 Congressional Elections

Candidate	Frei, 1964	Christian Democrats, 1965	Christian Democrats, 1969
Tomic, 1970	.53	.50	.64
Alessandri, 1970	.67	.31	.18

SOURCE: Calculated from electoral returns from the Dirección del Registro Electoral, Santiago, Chile.

ing the ambiguities of their centrist position, would have preferred Alessandri over Allende. This is vividly illustrated by the results of a survey taken shortly before the election and reported in table 13. Respondents were asked which candidates they would not vote for under any circumstances. As the table shows, 56.6 percent of those surveyed rejected the Allende candidacy, as opposed to 43.7 percent against Tomic and 40.1 percent against Alessandri. From the table we can deduce that 46 percent of the lower socioeconomic group would refuse to vote for the "popular" candidate, and only 48 percent would refuse to vote for the candidate identified with the economic elite. The latter group was clearer in its preferences, with 74 percent rejecting the Allende candidacy and only 22 percent rejecting the Alessandri candidacy. Allende simply would not have received a majority of the vote in a two-way race. The sharp polarization of the Chilean political system which was so clearly apparent in the 1970 vote is further underscored by the survey data presented in table 14. Voters were asked their reasons for refusing to vote for any one of the three candidates. Large proportions of the respondents rejected the candidates on the extremes for ideological reasons. Thus 61 percent of those rejecting Allende and 48 percent of those rejecting Alessandri cited unfavorable characteristics of the candidate's ideological posture. By contrast, only 9 percent of those rejecting the centrist candidate gave ideological reasons.

A brief analysis of the correlates of the 1970 presidential vote with several indicators of the urban and rural working class provides a further understanding of the different appeals of each of the candidates. The strongest simple correlations are the negative ones between the vote for Allende and agricultural workers (-.48) and the positive one between the Popular Unity candidate and miners (.50). Though table 15 shows that the president also did better than his adversaries among sectors of the urban working class, both the simple correlations and partial regression coefficients are substantially weaker. Nevertheless, the table does reveal a clear contrast in the base of support for Allende and his two contenders and a substantial similarity in the voting base of the two losing candidates. Both Tomic and Alessandri were strong in the rural areas. Analysis of scattergrams reveals that the stronger correlation between rural votes and Tomic than between rural votes and Alessandri is somewhat misleading. Alessandri in 1970 still had a clear edge over Tomic in

ble 13. **Percentage of Voters, by Socioeconomic Group, Refusing to Vote for Allende, Tomic, or essandri in 1970 under Any Circumstance**

CANDIDATE

	Allende		Tomic		Alessandri		Total	
Socioeconomic Group	Number of Responses	%	Number of Responses	%	Number of Responses	%	Number of Responses	%
Upper	89	73.6	61	50.4	27	22.3	121	12.0
Middle	239	66.4	140	38.9	124	34.4	360	35.8
Lower	241	45.9	239	43.8	253	48.2	525	52.2
Total	569	56.6	440	43.7	404	40.1	1,006	100.0

SOURCE: Sales-Reyes Survey, July–August 1970. The author is grateful to James Prothro and Patricio aparro for making the results of the survey available to him.
NOTE: The number of responses and the total number in sample do not agree since some respondents ected more than one candidate.

areas with the highest percentage of agricultural workers. However, since his support was also stronger in some communities with few agricultural workers, the correlation coefficient is slightly smaller. At the same time, the Left had made some inroads in communities with high concentrations of industrial workers. Even so, electoral analysis of the 1970 election shows that the social base of party politics in Chile remained quite heterogeneous. Indicators of the urban working class explain 36, 26, and 19 percent of the variance in the vote for Allende, Alessandri, and Tomic, respectively.

The Allende triumph drew international attention, not only because it represented the first free election of a Marxist head of government firmly committed to a fundamental transformation of his country's existing socioeconomic order but also because of the new government's promise to institute its revolutionary transformations in accord with Chilean constitutional and legal precepts. Indeed, Allende would refer to his experiment as one ranking in importance with the Russian Revolution. In a different historical context, Chile would pioneer in the establishment of a second model for the construction of a Socialist society, a model based not on the violent destruction of the old order

Table 14. **Percentage of Respondents Rejecting the Candidacies of Allende, Tomic, or Alessandri in 1970 on Ideological Grounds**

JUSTIFICATIONS

Candidate	Ideological	%	Non-ideological	%	Total Number of Responses
Allende	346	61.0	222	39.0	569
Tomic	38	8.6	402	91.4	440
Alessandri	194	48.0	210	52.0	404

SOURCE: Same as table 13.

Table 15. Simple and Partial Correlations between the Vote for Presidential Candidates in 1970 and Indicators of Working Classes

Nonagricultural Working Class	Allende		Alessandri		Tomic	
	r	Beta	r	Beta	r	Beta
Miners	.50	.45	−.47	−.45	−.31	−.27
Industrial artisans and workers	.25	.14	−.17	−.11	−.19	−.10
Urban wage laborers	.30	.12	−.19	−.05	−.28	−.16
Domestic and personal service workers	.10	.04	−.03	−.01	−.10	−.04
Office workers	.31	.23	−.17	−.10	−.31	−.27
Commercial workers and salespeople	.13	−.06	−.09	.04	−.09	.09
	R.60	R^2.36	R.51	R^2.26	R.44	R^2.19
Agricultural workers	−.48		.31		.39	

SOURCE: Calculated from 1970 census data and electoral data from the Dirección del Registro Electoral, Santiago, Chile.

but on its peaceful replacement according to democratic, pluralist, and libertarian traditions.[34]

Salvador Allende's stand would immediately raise the issue of whether a minority candidate committed to fundamental change would actually rule or would have to settle for merely reigning. The Congress was dominated by the Christian Democrats and the Right, and after the reforms of 1970 it was more of a confrontational than an accommodationist body. Key institutions such as the Contraloría and the courts were outside the executive chain of command. Indeed, Allende's "victory" led to an even more immediate question as to whether he would be allowed to take office in the first place. The Chilean constitution specified that if no candidate received an absolute majority of the votes, the actual election of the president had to take place in the Congress. A coalition which had failed to form before the election could very well be structured in the congressional arena.

In assessing the political climate of the country and the potential for the formation of the coalition that would enable Allende to take office and actually rule, it is important to specify more clearly the concrete dimensions and manifestations of polarized politics by identifying the positions of major political groups in Chilean society. In so doing, reference will not be made to the myriad individual issues which any society faces, but to two fundamental and overriding matters which Chile confronted in 1970: commitment to the ongoing socioeconomic order and commitment to the institutions and procedures of Chile's long-standing political democracy. These were general questions, often more symbolic than substantive and not easily disaggregated, which nevertheless involved extremely high stakes having to do with the survival of rules of the game themselves.

As noted above, Allende took a position on both, arguing that radical change could be instituted without disturbing the procedures of Chilean democracy. However, only a small fraction of the political elites strongly supported both values. This is the case because it is extremely difficult to isolate support for the rules and procedures of democratic politics from institutions and socioeconomic structures which have been long identified with the same rules. For some, the dismantling of the old order meant that the rules and procedures that permitted the dismantling would lose their legitimacy. Their stake in the social and economic benefits of the status quo was more important than their stake in democratic rules and procedures. By contrast, other factions placed greater value on the destruction of the old order than on the rules of the game which were thought to perpetuate the status quo. A second set of actors may have placed a high value on the rules and procedures but were equally divided on the desirability of change in the institutional and economic order. Support for rules and procedures is severely tested as the other value is put in jeopardy.

Figure 2 summarizes the placement of key Chilean political parties and groups on these two dimensions: support for rules and procedures and support for institutions. As the figure suggests, in 1970 those groups could be divided into anti-rules and pro-rules groups.

It is clear that in 1970 there were two different kinds of disloyal groups fulfilling Juan Linz's definition of those "willing to abandon competitive politics between parties and civil liberties required to maintain competition."[35] The first group rejected the prevailing socioeconomic order. It was made up primarily of the Movement of the Revolutionary Left (MIR). The MIR believed that the only way a Socialist society could be brought about was through a violent uprising of peasants and workers. This group was skeptical of the Allende candidacy and only reluctantly gave it support, signaling at the same time that they would continue their effort to organize and provoke a real confrontation as soon as possible. They presented a challenge from the Left to the proposition that change could come about through legal channels. The MIR position was shared by a rather sizable element of Allende's own party, the Socialists. Shortly before the election, this faction gained control of the party and made it clear that in the final analysis the transformation of the system would be achieved not by playing along with bourgeois elements but by pushing for a fundamental confrontation.[36] Both groups stressed the importance of bringing about a Socialist society and creating a new man. Allende's fundamental premise—that Chile could institute a Socialist order within the framework of democratic legality—was severely challenged by important elements within his own party.

The second group of disloyal elements came from the small sector of the

Commitment to Socioeconomic Order

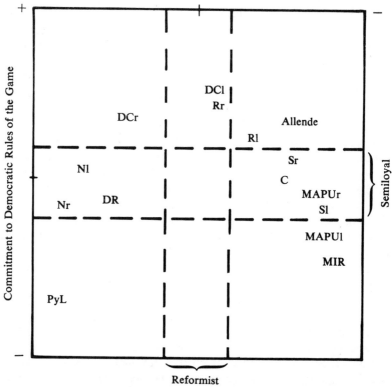

Reformist

LEGEND: r = rightist; l = leftist; DC = Democracia Cristiana; DR = Democracia Radical; N = Nacional; PyL = Patria y Libertad; S = Socialista; C = Comunista; MAPU = Movimiento de Acción Popular Unitario; MIR = Movimiento de Izquierda Revolucionario.

Figure 2. Placement of Key Political Groups in 1970 on Two Dimensions: Commitment to the Socioeconomic Order and Commitment to the Democratic Rules of the Game

society which had clearly reaped enormous social and economic rewards from the status quo. As members of the economic Right, many were openly hostile to Chilean democratic institutions and from the outset sought to bar the election of Allende or forcefully remove him from office. In general, the disloyal Right counted on the support of only a handful of activists in late 1970. They were powerful, and they counted among their number elements within the armed forces with close links to U.S. intelligence sources intent on destroying the Popular Unity government. The disloyal rightist ranks would swell considerably as time went by, drawing individuals not only from the wealthy economic groups but also from middle-class and military sectors. Much of the leadership of the nation's industrial and commercial federations were clearly more sympathetic toward the antidemocratic Right than they were toward the more traditional political Right, which had a greater stake in partisan politics. From the outset, then, it was clear that on both sides there were elements whose commitment to their preferred socioeconomic order was greater than their commitment to the democratic process.

The pro-rules group was composed of elements who were loyal to the principles underlying the democratic rules of the game. However, this group was also sharply divided on the desirability of a radical transformation of the socioeconomic structures of society. The president, who had been a member of the Chilean Congress for decades and was a former president of the senate and an author of numerous pieces of social welfare legislation, was joined in his belief that fundamental change could be achieved legally by several other groups in the Popular Unity coalition. First and foremost among these was the Communist party, which argued strongly that the only possible strategy in Chile was a gradual consolidation of power within the framework of traditional institutions. The Radical party, which included outstanding Chilean political personalities such as Senators Luis Bossay and Alberto Baltra, was also convinced that Chilean socialism could become a reality without revolutionary violence. The moderate sector of the Socialist party, of which Senator Aniceto Rodriguez was a prominent spokesman, concurred with that thesis, as did some elements in the progressive wing of the Christian Democrats, including Radomiro Tomic. It must be noted, however, that even within these groups there were substantial differences. The Communists, and, to a degree, Allende himself, argued that eventually the process would lead to the creation of new institutions and procedures. Fundamental transformation would be political as well as socioeconomic. Indeed, even on the question of the future viability of traditional electoral procedures, the Communists were hesitant.[37] By contrast, other groups, including many Radicals and Socialists, were more interested in the inauguration of fundamental socioeconomic changes without the radical transformation of Chile's social democratic political framework. The progressive Christian Democrats envisioned a different kind of socialism, one with much less central control than the socialism envisioned by Communists.[38] While desiring more popular input, they too were more committed to the main outline of traditional institutional arrangements.

Though there were important divisions between leaders and groups who, in broad terms, shared the president's goals, there was a sharp division between them and those sectors who believed in the institutions and rules of the game but were antagonistic to accelerated social and economic transformations. This sector was made up of those elements of the National party who had a long history of political involvement and took great pride in the democratic rules their forefathers had fashioned. Most of them held comfortable positions in commercial, industrial, and agricultural circles, and feared the further erosions in their status which would result from continued challenges to the capitalist system. Many Christian Democrats, identified with the more conservative policies of the last year of the Frei administration, shared these views. Though perhaps more willing than the Nationals to consolidate some reforms, such as those initiated in the countryside, they were much less willing to accept fundamental challenge to a progressive capitalism than were the moderate sectors of the Popular Unity coalition or the progressive sectors of their own party.[39]

The pro-rules sectors were under enormous pressure because of the inherent contradictions within their own amorphous ranks. Those favoring dramatic change faced the clear prospect of having their hopes thwarted. Those favoring the economic or political status quo faced the possibility of loss of privilege and the erosion of traditional institutions. Broad sectors of both groups were capable of falling into the category of "disloyal opposition" as their attachment to the rules faltered. Both would be tested by the constraints of the Chilean system and by the pressures of increasingly mobilized sectors. Eventually the contradictions, coupled with the strong pressure from anti-rules groups, would lead to a characterization of the tradeoffs as zero-sum tradeoffs. And yet Allende, and many others, were confident at the outset that history was on their side, and that it would not be necessary to choose between established rules and a fervent commitment to greater social justice.

This analysis suggests that the number of politically relevant groups and leaders who shared Allende's position on both major issues was very small. Ideological polarization was at an all-time high. It also suggests the enormous predicament which Allende faced in the Chilean Congress. To be elected president he needed a majority, and yet with eighty-three seats in both houses his coalition was eighteen seats short of a majority.

But the Nationals and Radical Democrats, intent on stopping Allende, commanded only forty-three seats in the legislature, a number far too small to engineer the election of Jorge Alessandri. The divided Christian Democrats at the Center of the political spectrum held the balance of power with their seventy-four seats.[40] The pressure on the Christian Democrats was enormous, not only from within the country but from the United States.[41]

Already, U.S. corporations, with the tacit support of the U.S. government, had added their weight to the financial panic instigated by Chilean big business as soon as Allende won the election. In the most blatant intervention in the history of Chilean politics, President Nixon ordered the CIA to stop Allende's election. It soon became clear to U.S. agents, however, that it would not be possible to bribe Christian Democratic legislators. Furthermore, President Frei would have nothing to do with a scheme to have the Congress vote for Alessandri with the understanding that Alessandri would then resign, thus paving the way for a new election in which Frei would be eligible to run for office again. With the approval of the top authorities of the United States government, the CIA then tried to convince key figures of the Chilean military to stage a coup. When the pro-American general, René Schneider, commander in chief of the army, refused to think about such an alternative, foreign and domestic conspirators kidnapped the general in the mistaken hope that the act would produce a coup.[42] In the first political assassination of a prominent Chilean leader since 1837, Schneider was shot to death by his would-be kidnappers. The plot clearly backfired, as most of the conspirators were identified and convicted. President Frei and president-elect Allende marched side by side in the funeral cortege attended by a broad spectrum of civilian and military leadership.

The struggle within the Christian Democratic party over the election of Allende was intense. Tomic, the losing candidate, had already gone on record supporting the Allende victory. Shortly after the ballots were counted, he had embraced his "old friend" and pledged full support. But even though the Tomic wing of the party controlled the more important leadership positions, distrust of Allende was pervasive. A decision to vote for Allende threatened the weak unity of the party.

The impasse was finally resolved when Allende agreed to support a constitutional amendment that would require him to respect civil liberties, elections, and freedom of the press, all of which had been understood to be cornerstones of Chilean democracy for generations. The so-called *Estatuto de Garantía* (Statute of Guarantees) was a vivid illustration of the serious polarization of Chilean politics and the severe erosion of the traditional rules of the game. Those rules in the final analysis are based on a degree of trust, and the need to extract a formal declaration from Allende that he would preserve the constitution showed the deterioration of confidence between political leaders who had been close for decades and for whom a respect for the rules of the game had been implicit. It was also clear evidence of fear that the game of winning support at the expense of other sectors, which had been accelerated during the Christian Democratic period, would continue with renewed strength.

Unlike the Pact of Punto Fijo in Venezuela, which marked the beginning of a period of détente between antagonistic groups and was a mutual agreement to respect the outcome of elections, the Estatuto de Garantía, extracted as a condition for political support, marked a breakdown in mutual understanding signaling the fragility of Chilean institutions.[43] Allende began his administration in an atmosphere of profound crisis. Financial panic, political confrontation, and the resolute attempts by military conspirators and foreign intelligence agents to prevent him from coming to office did not augur well for the government. Many individuals openly questioned the legitimacy of the system which made his election possible, and others, while providing support, showed a profound distrust in the new president's good faith and a real fear for the future of the country's institutions.

3.

The Move to a Socialist Society and the Erosion of the Political Center

Upon his inauguration, Allende moved swiftly and with great political skill to enact a program which he hoped would eventually lead to a socialist society with genuine popular control over economic and political life.[1] His early programs of distributing milk to children and the relaxed style of the *"compañero presidente"* who would mix with the population in his shirt-sleeves brought significant personal support.[2] The Christian Democrats continued their tacit support by agreeing to vote for Popular Unity leadership in one of the houses of Congress. Allende, a genuine idealist, was sure that he would quickly overcome his minority election as the people became convinced that his government was a true popular government. When Regis Debray asked him what he would do if the Congress blocked some of his proposals, he did not hesitate to answer that he would call a plebiscite to override congressional opposition.[3]

The economic policy of the Allende administration involved a four-pronged strategy of income redistribution, expansion of government programs and services, state control of key industries, and extension of land reform. The ultimate goal was to transform class and property relations and to institute a new economic development scheme along Socialist lines.

The policy of income redistribution was aimed not so much at reducing differentials between categories of wage and salary earners as at increasing labor's share of the national income in relationship to the private corporate and *rentier* sectors of the economy. Chilean policy-makers believed that this policy was perfectly viable in conventional economic terms. By increasing income, new demand would be generated, in turn inducing a rise in production in a sluggish economy operating well below capacity. Since much of the new demand would come from low income wage earners, it would spur demand in the labor-intensive sector of the economy, which produced the bulk of the goods consumed by low income people. Unemployment would be further reduced, spurring production.[4]

The fact that the economic policy was based on standard economic calculations does not mean that government officials and planners were oblivious to the political consequences of the strategy. Quite to the contrary, they were hopeful that the potential risk of accelerated income distribution would be offset by clear political gains for the Popular Unity coalition. Economic objectives were not sought merely as an end in themselves, but as tools to broaden the admittedly weak support which Allende had received in his narrow electoral victory. Pedro Vuskovick, the minister of economy and principal architect of the economic program, stressed forcefully that the basic program of the government was not merely reformist but revolutionary. He added:

if that is our starting point, what is involved in economic policy is not a set of technical problems, but rather an essentially political problem, serving primarily, and that is its central objective, as an instrument to broaden and consolidate the positions of power of the workers . . . economic policy is determined both by a desire to realize an economic program fully and completely and by a need to secure in the economic sphere the appropriate political conditions to develop the overall program. That is the reason for the simultaneous existence of programmatic and strategic objectives in economic policy.[5]

In sum, it must be stressed that the policies followed by the Allende government in the crucial first year were not simply a response to uncontrolled popular pressure for a greater share of the finite goods of Chilean society but were the result of a deliberate policy with clear economic and political objectives. Certainly the Popular Unity government raised great expectations, and its policies would subsequently encourage ever-increasing pressures. The fact is, however, that income redistribution and price controls were set in motion as a concerted and calculated policy initiated from above.

The record shows that the process of income distribution exceeded governmental goals. The government raised the basic wage by 66.6 percent and the basic monthly salary by 35 percent. By July of 1971 average income per employee had increased by 54.9 percent rather than the 40 percent to 45 percent programmed.[6]

Income redistribution was accompanied by a dramatic increase in government spending, particularly on social services such as housing, education, health, and sanitation. By the end of 1971, fiscal expenditures had increased 70 percent, from 19 to 33 billion *escudos*. Ten billion of this amount was financed by Central Bank credits, as opposed to only 1.8 billion the previous year. At the same time, as table 16 shows, credit expanded substantially; the public sector's share of total bank credit increased from less than one-third to almost 60 percent.[7] For the twelve-month period between December 1970 and December 1971, the money in circulation increased by 110.5 percent as the government sought to meet the financial demands of its new programs and obligations.[8]

Table 16. Total Amount of Credit Granted by the Banking System, December 1970–December 1971 (millions of escudos)

	Public Sector			Private Sector	Total
	Treasury	Other	Total		
End of December 1970	916	1,152	2,068	6,777	8,845
End of July 1971	6,487	2,634	9,121	8,512	17,633
End of December 1971	9,301	6,814	16,115	10,785	26,900

SOURCE: Banco Central, *Boletín Mensual*, no. 537, November 1972, p. 1362; cited in Stefan de Vylder, *Allende's Chile: The Political Economy of the Rise and Fall of the Unidad Popular* (Cambridge: Cambridge University Press, 1976), p. 57.

Initially, the Popular Unity government's economic policies had very positive effects. In 1971 the gross domestic product increased by 8.6 percent, the best single year in decades, with moderate to strong increases in all major sectors.[9] Unemployment declined as employment in areas such as construction, public utilities, manufacturing, and services increased 11.7 percent, 7.6 percent, 7.1 percent, and 5.1 percent, respectively.[10] Increased production led to increased demand, primarily for basic goods such as agricultural products. Agricultural production did register an increase of 8.6 percent in crop-farming and 1.8 percent in livestock production. This increase, however, was not enough to meet the burgeoning demand, and the government was forced to increase its imports of foreign goods sharply. In the short run such a measure was feasible because of the ample reserves which had accumulated due to the rise in copper prices in the last years of the Frei administration. Finally, the ability of the economy to respond to government stimulation meant that inflation actually dropped from 34.9 percent in 1970 to 22.1 percent in 1971.[11]

The government also moved swiftly in its effort to create a Socialist economy. By nationalizing major industries, government planners hoped to be able to channel profit not only into further investment but also into subsidies for government programs. Likewise, nationalization of the banks would give the government control over credit for the same purposes. Both banks and industries were taken over by purchasing shares of their stock or by employing existing legislation permitting authorities to intervene in a firm which for some reason was not providing essential services.[12] Workers sympathetic to the Popular Unity coalition often forced a plant or enterprise to cease operations, opening the way for government takeover. By December 1971 the number of industrial establishments controlled by the state had risen from thirty-one to sixty-two, not including thirty-nine more under government seizure.[13] A major accomplishment for the government was the nationalization of the United States copper interests after the Chilean Congress, controlled by the opposition, unanimously approved the necessary legislation. Though nationalization of the copper industry would aggravate the dispute between the government and the foreign enterprises, it must be stressed that many other foreign firms were taken over on mutually agreeable terms.[14]

The takeover of banks and business enterprises generally proceeded without much violence. The opposite was true in agricultural areas, where landowners resisted government expropriation or workers took over the land. Members of the MIR made significant inroads in some rural areas, providing organizational support and, in some cases, arms for rural confrontations. As table 17 shows, rural strikes continued to increase in 1971, but there was a real explosion of land seizures, which increased by 180 percent over 1970. The administration was reluctant to repress such activities and thus tacitly encouraged them, asserting that disputes occurred in only .02 percent of all properties.[15] Spurred in part by farm workers, the Allende government seized over 1,300 properties during its first year, 300 more than the number expropriated in the six years of the preceding administration.[16]

Government planners, hoping for popular approval of their policies, were not disappointed with the outcome of the first nationwide test of political strength after the 1970 election, which was the 1971 election of municipal councils. As table 18 shows, the Popular Unity parties received a slightly higher percentage of the total vote than did the opposition parties. In a slightly smaller electorate than the one participating in the previous year's presidential election (despite an increase in registration, which included for the first time illiterates and eighteen–twenty-one-year-olds), the opposition parties received 486,980 fewer votes, while the government gained 307,375 votes. In particular, President Allende's own Socialist party did extremely well, with an increase in support of 95 percent over the 1967 municipal election. This compared favorably to the increase of 83 percent which President Frei's party had gained in the 1967 municipal elections by comparison with the 1963 contest. Whereas the 1967 election had given the opposition a clear advantage, by 1971 the Left had pulled abreast, with a net increase of nine percent over the previous municipal election.[17] Preliminary analysis of the 1971 municipal election suggests that the increase in support came from diverse sectors of the active population. As will be analyzed more closely below, the social bases of the vote in 1971 for all the Popular Unity parties did not change dramatically with respect to the vote for Allende in 1970.

Table 17. Number of Rural Conflicts Resulting in Strikes or Land Seizures (Tomas), 1967–71

	1967	1968	1969	1970	1971
Strikes	693	648	1,127	1,580	1,758
Tomas	9	26	148	456	1,278
Total	702	674	1,275	2,036	3,036

SOURCE: Stefan de Vylder, *Allende's Chile: The Political Economy of the Rise and Fall of the Unidad Popular* (Cambridge: Cambridge University Press, 1976), p. 204.

Table 18. Results of Municipal Elections, 1967 and 1971

Party	1967 Number of Votes	%	1971 Number of Votes	%
Popular Unity				
Socialists	324,965	13.9	663,367	22.3
Communists	346,105	14.8	477,862	16.9
Radicals [a]	252,640	10.8	228,426	8.1
Social Democrats [b]	17,457	0.1	38,054	1.3
Total	941,167	40.0	1,377,709	48.6
Opposition				
Christian Democrats	834,810	35.6	729,398	25.7
Nationals	334,656	14.3	513,074	18.1
Radical Democrats [a]	124,434	5.3	110,021	3.9
Padena [b]	38,859		13,487	0.5
Total	1,332,759	57.0	1,365,980	48.2
Others, blank and void	69,361	3.0	128,967	3.0
Grand Total	2,343,287	100.0	2,835,402	100.0
Total registered	3,073,992		3,792,682	
Percentage of abstentions	23.7		23.7	

SOURCE: Calculated from data available in the Dirección del Registro Electoral, Santiago, Chile.

[a] The Democracia Radical had not been created in 1967. The Radical vote was arbitrarily divided between Radicals and Radical Democrats, assuming that the relative strength of the two factions was the same in 1967 as it was in 1971, the first election after the split.

[b] The Social Democrats and PADENA, which were combined in 1967, have been arbitrarily separated, assuming that the relative strength of the parties was the same as it was in the 1969 congressional election, the first election after the split.

One of the most important characteristics of the 1971 vote is that it reflected further political polarization. Because the electorate perceived the contest to be between a Popular Unity coalition and a more status quo-oriented opposition, it threw more of its support to the two parties on the extremes, the Socialists and the Nationals. All of the centrist parties, including the Christian Democrats and the two Radical fragments, lost support in absolute terms with respect to the previous election. Their combined percentage of the vote declined from 52 percent to 40 percent.

Though the short-term policies of the Popular Unity coalition contributed to economic and political success in 1971, it would be misleading to imply that serious difficulties did not surface in that same year, difficulties that presaged new problems. Government economists were aware of the potentially explosive consequences of an overstimulated economy. As Minister Vuskovic himself noted in an October 1971 seminar, two very serious consequences of government policy were the drastic reduction in investment and the almost complete depletion of foreign reserves.[18] Despite increases in public investment, domestic investment outside of construction dropped 71.3 percent.[19]

The policy of accommodating demand with imports resulted in a critical shortage of foreign reserves as copper prices dropped and production in the largest copper mines decreased. The $343.4 million in reserves the country had in 1970 had dwindled to $32.3 million by December of 1971.[20] The priority given to the importation of foodstuffs, which rose from 14 percent to 24 percent of total imports, meant a corresponding decline in other items, including a decline of 22 percent in imported machinery.[21] These figures suggest that by the end of 1971, increased demand stimulated by the government had already reached a level which exceeded the short-term capability of domestic production and import capacity. Vuskovic himself underscored this, noting that "bottlenecks" could only be avoided by increased investments and production. He also warned that because of these potential difficulties "it is difficult to visualize for next year a policy of wage increases with the same likelihood that those increases would not be translated, automatically, into higher prices."[22] He further envisioned a period of consolidation rather than expansion of the income gains of 1971.

Unfortunately for the government and for the country, the year 1972 would not be a year of consolidation, and the economic picture would contrast unfavorably with that of 1971. By July 1972, as table 19 shows, inflation had increased sharply to 45.9 percent and by the end of the year had quadrupled to a record high of 163.4 percent. By December 1972 Chile's reserve situation showed a net deficit of $288.7 million and its balance of payments deficit had increased four-fold over the previous year to $538 million.[23] Bottlenecks developed at an ever-increasing rate as black market operations and hoarding

Table 19. Yearly Rates of Inflation, December 1970–September 1973

Period	Percentage Increase in Prices
December 1970–December 1971	22.1
June 1971–June 1972	40.1
July 1971–July 1972	45.9
August 1971–August 1972	77.2
September 1971–September 1972	114.3
October 1971–October 1972	142.9
November 1971–November 1972	149.8
December 1971–December 1972	163.4
January 1972–January 1973	180.3
February 1972–February 1973	174.1
March 1972–March 1973	183.3
April 1972–April 1973	195.5
May 1972–May 1973	238.4
June 1972–June 1973	283.4
July 1972–July 1973	323.2
August 1972–August 1973	303.6
September 1972–September 1973	286.0
October 1972–October 1973	528.4
April 1973–April 1974	746.2

SOURCE: Instituto Nacional de Estadística, mimeographed reports.

became common practices and production was unable to keep pace with demands for essential items. In order to prevent a dramatic cutback in government programs, money was printed at an even faster rate; consequently, by 1972 the percentage of the budget covered by emissions had increased from 30 or 40 percent over the previous year.[24]

The Popular Unity government's problems were compounded by sharp cutbacks in international aid and credit. The hostility which greeted the Allende election victory in U.S. governmental and financial circles was soon translated into a policy of cutting off support for the Popular Unity government. The Chilean nationalization of the copper industry further hardened this policy. U.S. officials used their influence with international lending agencies such as the World Bank and the Inter-American Development Bank to cut off aid. The World Bank eliminated all new aid and the IDB approved only small loans to private organizations. At the same time the U.S. Export Import Bank denied credit for purchasing U.S. jetliners, and governmental aid and loan programs were discontinued. Private banks, whose short-term credits are often vital in international transactions, also reduced loan programs with the Chilean government.[25] During the Frei administration, an average of $300 million in short-term credits was available to Chile. By 1972, that figure had dwindled to $30 million.[26] Table 20 summarizes the actions of major U.S. and international lending and aid agencies before and during the Popular Unity administration.

It is crucial to stress that in absolute terms the decline of aid to Chile did not represent a severe cutback in resources. But given the sharp drop in copper prices, the dramatic increases in the importation of food, and the huge indebtedness which the Allende government inherited from its predecessor, restrictions on aid and credits seriously complicated the government's predicament. This was particularly true for aid from U.S. sources. Since tools and machinery of U.S. origin were so important to the Chilean economy, the difficulties which Chile faced in obtaining spare parts contributed to dislocations in the productive sector. For example, in the transportation sector, the value of machinery and equipment of U.S. origin dropped from $152.6 million in 1970 to $110 million in 1971, and by late 1972, according to some estimates, 30 percent of private buses, 33 percent of state buses, and 21 percent of all taxis were out of commission due to lack of parts. One estimate is that the value of the U.S. share of total Chilean imports dropped from 37.2 percent in 1970 to about 10 percent in 1972.[27] Though the Chilean government was able to establish commercial links with other countries and obtain alternative credits, these were often tied to specific items and projects and could not completely substitute for American-made products. A dramatic indication of this was the Chilean government's decision in 1972 to purchase a Boeing jetliner with cash rather than accept credit to purchase two Soviet airliners which would have necessitated a complete revamping of the whole support and maintenance infrastructure.[28]

Table 20. Foreign Aid to Chile from U.S. Government Agencies and International Institutions—Total of Loans and Grants (in millions of dollars)

FISCAL YEAR

	1953–61	1962	1963	1964	1965	1966	1967	1968	1969	1970	1971	1972	1973	1974
Total U.S. economic aid	339.7	169.8	85.3	127.1	130.4	111.9	260.4	97.1	80.8	29.6	8.6	7.4	3.8	9.8
AID	76.4	142.7	41.3	78.9	99.5	93.2	15.5	57.9	35.4	18.0	1.5	1.0	.8	5.3
Food for Peace	94.2	6.6	22.0	26.9	14.2	14.4	7.9	23.0	15.0	7.2	6.3	5.9	2.5	3.2
Export-Import Bank	169.0	.8	16.2	15.3	8.2	.1	234.6	14.2	28.7	3.3	—	1.6	3.1	98.1[a]
Total U.S. military aid	41.8	17.8	30.6	9.0	9.9	10.1	4.1	7.8	11.8	.8	5.7	12.3	15.0	15.9
Total U.S. economic and military aid	381.5	187.6	115.9	136.1	140.3	122.0	264.5	104.9	91.8	30.4	14.3[b]	21.3[b]	21.9	123.8[b]
Total international organizations[c]	135.4	18.7	31.2	41.4	12.4	72.0	93.8	19.4	49.0	76.4	15.4	28.2	9.4	111.2
IBRD (World Bank)	95.2	—	—	22.6	4.4	2.7	60.0	—	11.6	19.3	—	—	—	13.5
Inter-American Development Bank	5.7	15.1	24.4	16.6	4.9	62.2	31.0	16.5	31.9	45.6	12.0	2.1	5.2	97.3

SOURCE: "U.S. Overseas Loans and Grants, Obligations and Loan Authorizations, 1 July 1945 to 30 June 1971," pp. 40, 179; and "1 July 1945 to 30 June 1974," pp. 39, 175. Prepared by Statistics and Reports Division, Office of Financial Management, Agency for International Development, and printed in U.S., Senate, "Hearings, before the Select Committee to Study Governmental Operations with respect to Intelligence Activities," vol. 7 (4 and 5 December 1975), p. 181.

[a] Includes $57 million from the Export-Import Bank and $41.1 million from other sources.

[b] Total per chart plus Export-Import Bank.

[c] U.S. contributions to International organizations included above; therefore U.S. aid and international aid should not be added.

Because of the dependent nature of the Chilean economy, the dwindling of the Chilean government's international reserve position made the country extremely vulnerable to international retaliation. Though Chile's economic difficulties cannot be attributed solely to an international economic "blockade," that blockade did contribute to a spiral of increasing economic difficulties.

These mounting economic difficulties soon posed a substantial political threat to the government. In December 1971, middle-class women staged the much-publicized march of the empty pots. By August 1972 it was clear that the government's economic policies were seriously affecting the upper and middle classes. Table 21 presents the results of a survey taken in August 1972. The survey reveals that 99 percent of the upper classes felt that it was difficult to buy supplies—a feeling shared by 77 percent of the middle classes. While the policy of the government was clearly perceived as threatening by approximately 60 percent of the population, 75 percent of the lower classes felt that it was now easier to obtain goods. These figures reflect considerable discontent in the petit bourgeois group that the Popular Unity government had considered important to the success of its program.

In the political sphere, the government experienced some reversals after the 1971 municipal election. Popular Unity candidates were defeated by a united opposition in three out of four congressional by-elections. In April 1972, the government's candidate was defeated in the crucial election for the rectorship of the University of Chile. The results showed that the Popular Unity lost ground not only among the usually conservative sectors of the faculties but also among segments of the university that had for years provided majorities to Marxist candidates. Finally, in the first fully democratic popular elections of the Chilean Labor Federation, the Christian Democrats did surprisingly well, actually winning majorities in one of the large copper companies which had traditionally selected leftist labor leaders. At the same time, the government found that its plans to enact a unicameral legislature and popular courts were stalled, while the effort to institute a system of genuine worker participation in industrial decision-making, with a few interesting exceptions, never really got off the ground.

Further political difficulties for the Allende administration arose in confrontations with other institutions and forces in the complex Chilean institutional arena. On several occasions government actions were stymied by objections from the Contraloría or from the courts. However, the most ominous confrontation was posed by the opposition in Congress. In his first year, Allende had shuffled his cabinet only once, to resolve internal disputes within his coalition. By the end of 1972, he had instituted two full and six partial cabinet changes involving seventeen ministerial posts—several in response to attempts by the Congress to impeach his ministers. In January and again in July of 1972 his minister of the interior was impeached by Congress. Congress

Table 21. Response to the Survey Question, "In Your Opinion, is Buying Essential Products at This Time for Your Home Easy or Difficult?"

| | SOCIOECONOMIC GROUPS | | | |
	Upper	Middle	Lower	Total
Easy	1%	17%	75%	47%
Difficult	99	77	19	48
Neither	0	6	6	5

SOURCE: *Ercilla*, 13–19 September 1972, p. 10.

used its veto power to deny tax increases which could have helped to alleviate the fiscal crisis. In February of 1972 both houses of Congress approved legislation that called for a constitutional amendment to regulate the areas of the economy. If adopted, it would mean that Allende would have to modify significantly his program of creating a Socialist sector of the economy.[29] The amendment would permit the takeover of industries only by legislative approval and, because of a retroactive provision, would require the executive to place in the hands of Congress the entire policy of his first months in office. Passage of the provision on the economy was to engender the most significant confrontation of the Allende regime. Its importance lies in the fact that it marked the clear breakdown of the tenuous centrist consensus which had enabled Allende to reach the presidency. What happened? How did an auspicious beginning turn so sour? Why was the government unable to consolidate the gains of 1971? Why did the fragile Center collapse?

Internal and External Constraints: The Problem of a Minority Coalition Intent on Change in a Highly Polarized Society

The early failures of the Popular Unity government and the eventual breakdown of Chilean democracy cannot be explained by accusing one side or the other of destroying the system. It was not merely the result of erroneous economic policies or a deliberate strategy on the part of elements in the government to accelerate the collapse of bourgeois institutions. Nor was it simply the result of reactionary forces, aided and abetted from abroad, who sought to preserve privilege at all cost. Certainly these elements were present in varying degrees. But the breakdown of democracy in Chile must be understood in broader terms. It must be understood as the failure to structure a viable Center in a highly polarized society with strong centrifugal tendencies. As noted earlier, key sectors in both the government and the opposition were committed to the possibility of change within the context of ongoing institutional processes. But it was not only a matter of choice. Actions and decisions were subject to the powerful constraints and limitations of the ongoing system's electoral and institutional dimensions. Both those in the government and those in the opposition who were committed to a peaceful resolution of conflict were buffeted by pressures from both extremes. The pressure was so great that the long-term advantage of structuring working agreements was continously set aside in favor of the short-term requirement of preserving immediate political strength. The government found itself incapable of shifting away from its income distribution policies or imposing order on the working class for fear not only of the opposition but of rival elements within its own coalition. Its initiatives were blocked in the rambling bureaucracy and questioned by the courts, the Contraloría, and the Congress. The fundamental structural transformations it sought to achieve were blocked by a constitution it could not amend for lack of votes in Congress. Likewise, for the fragmented Christian Democrats, ideological pressures and electoral considerations, dictated by the continuous challenge of the National party for leadership of the opposition, made it increasingly difficult to continue with a policy of tacit support for the government. The politics of outbidding, as much within each coalition as between coalitions, carried the day.

It is crucial to stress that this process was a dialectical one. Government actions, taken to overcome political constraints and open opposition, often resulted in greater and more intense opposition, in turn forcing the government to take additional actions which could only worsen the political climate. The fragmentation of elites, the independence of a highly vocal and partisan media, the continuous mobilization of mass support by both camps and by elements within each camp added further to the confusion and made it hard to arrive at the minimum consensus necessary to preserve the regime. In time, many centrist elements on both sides would move increasingly into semiloyal or disloyal positions.

Does this mean that the outcome was inevitable? Though the political constraints provided the critical parameters defining the limits and potentials for political choice and action, it does not follow that the outcome was inevitable. In Chile there was room for choice. Class consciousness was not such that the working class in Chile would have settled for no less than total revolution—for surely compromise would have meant that. Neither were large segments of the middle class so reactionary that they would settle for only a Fascist government. At certain key junctures in the unfolding Chilean drama different choices would have led to different results, though as the process unfolded itself, and as polarization became more extreme, the range of the possible was dramatically reduced. It is the task of this section to analyze both the government and the opposition, pointing out some of their constraints and opportunities. Because of the unfolding evolution of a complex process, the analytical argument will of necessity be combined with a description of the changing parameters of the system over time.

The Popular Unity Government

Juan Linz has argued that many of the problems faced by governments during a crisis relate to their inability to solve major problems. Unsolvable problems are in part the responsibility of policy-makers themselves, who are unable to provide an adequate response due to a lack of means or knowledge, or the incompatibility of necessary actions with those that have greater priority.[30] The economic crisis during the Allende period clearly became the government's chief unsolvable problem. Though opposition groups must bear much of the blame for economic sabotage, government policies created strong reaction and its counterpolicies simply did not succeed in avoiding economic catastrophe.

The stark reality of the Allende years was that it proved to be politically impossible to cut back on the policy of increasing the income of poorer sectors of society and of those sectors affiliated with the Left. The strike at the El Salvador mine early in the Allende period, though resolved in the government's favor, presaged many more, including the crippling strike at El Teniente in the winter of 1973. What made the situation intolerable, however, was that wage increases for those sectors whose increases had traditionally been postponed were not accompanied by a parallel cutback in the portion of the national economic pie going to the more privileged groups. By February 1972 across-the-board wage increases were granted to make up for heightened inflation. Important groups such as the armed forces, radio operators, and Chuquicamata miners managed to get readjustments substantially higher than official inflation figures. By October 1972 wages and salaries for all but the wealthiest elements had increased by 99.8 percent over the previous year.[31] Like previous governments, the Popular Unity government did not succeed in deviating from the traditional policies of patronage and reajuste. "The income policy of 1971 was based on the principle of overall expansion rather than distribution. Quite consciously, the UP decided to favor not only the poor majority (which in percentage terms received a little more than average) but the comparatively well-to-do middle classes as well."[32] When the newly mobilized sectors sought their due on the same basis as everyone else, the Chilean economy was severely taxed.

The favorable predisposition of the government to the economic betterment of practically everyone in the society contributed to a dramatic rise in strike activity. Whereas in 1969 there were 977 strikes, in 1972 the figure had jumped to an all-time high of 3,287. In the first two years of the Allende government strike activity increased by 170 percent, far exceeding the increase of 45 percent in the 1964–66 period. As table 22 shows, strike activity far outstripped any new unionization. In fact, in 1972 the unionized industrial population continued to be slightly smaller than it had been in 1952. (See tables 7 and 9 for a comparison with earlier years.) A breakdown of this strike

Table 22. Growth of Industrial, Craft, and Agricultural Unions During the Popular Unity Years

Year	Number of Industrial Unions	Number of Members in Industrial Unions	Average Size of Industrial Unions	Number of Craft Unions	Number of Members in Craft Unions	Average Size of Craft Unions	Number of Agricultural Unions
1964	632	142,951	226.2	1,207	125,926	104.5	24
1970	1,440	197,651	137.3	2,569	239,323	93.2	510
1971	1,605	205,894	128.3	2,881	252,924	87.8	632
1972	1,781	213,777	120.0	3,511	282,181	80.4	709

SOURCE: For 1964, see tables 7 and 9. For 1970, see *Mensaje del Presidente ante el Congreso Pleno*, 21 M 1972, pp. 859, 860, and 861. For 1971 and 1972, see *Mensaje del Presidente ante el Congreso Pleno*, 21 M 1973, pp. 793 and 794. The author is grateful to Henry Landsberger for making these reports available to hi

activity shows that in 1971 the agricultural sector, with only 12.3 percent of the unions, experienced 38.6 percent of the strikes. By 1972, however, most of the strike activity had shifted to the urban areas. Strikes by public employees accounted for some of this shift, increasing from 132 in 1971 to 815 in 1972, a jump of 145 percent. In dialectical fashion, groups from all walks of life responded to government attempts to ameliorate their situation by making further demands.

There is little doubt that by 1972 mobilization had gotten out of hand, often to the chagrin of the president, who tried to obtain more discipline by cajoling the populace. Yet the government continued to encourage indiscipline by its policies. This was the case not only because of the goal of redistribution but also because many strikes were encouraged by government officials and Popular Unity political groups in order to accelerate the process of takeover of industries.

To many government officials, it seemed that the takeover of industries, spurred by worker initiatives, would in turn contribute to the solution of the problem of heightened demand. By controlling key sectors of the economy they would be able to make the decisions necessary to manage inflation and spur production. Table 23 provides information on interventions and requisitions, including temporary ones, through November 1972. These accelerated in times of political crisis such as late 1971 and September and October of 1972. By the end of 1972 approximately one-fourth of industrial production was in state hands.[33]

The trouble was that state intervention in industry posed unanticipated problems which aggravated rather than lessened the economic difficulties. Some were political and some were economic. Thus, the takeover was met by a strong and hostile reaction among both large and small businessmen and their allies. The vast majority were in no danger of government takeover. Nevertheless, they feared that they too would be expropriated. Sabotage and hoarding became the order of the day. In January 1972 the *Partido de Iz-*

Number of members in agricultural Unions	Average Size of Agricultural Unions	Number of Strikes	Number of Strikes per Union	Number of Workers on Strike	Number of Workers per Strike	Man-days Lost	Days per Strike per Worker	Year
1,658	69.1	564	.31	138,474	245	869,728	10.6	1964
14,112	223.7							1970
27,782	202.2	2,709	.52	304,530	112	1,414,313	4.6	1971
36,527	192.6	3,289	.55	397,142	121	1,654,151	4.2	1972

quierda Radical (PIR), still a member of the Popular Unity coalition, urged that the government issue a clear statement of its policy of economic regulation so as to permit small and middle-sized industries to return to normal operations. They noted that the uncertainty caused by the takeover of firms had led to an 8 percent decline in total investment and a 20 percent decline in private investment.[34] Sabotage from the Right, economic uncertainty, and disruption of plant operations contributed to production difficulties by the second year of Allende's term, compounding the problem of meeting demands.

But sabotage and labor indiscipline were only part of the problem. Many firms had been mismanaged or neglected, and on entry into the public sector they proved to be more of a burden than an asset.[35] Furthermore, and ironically, the very policy of wage increases and price freezes which were to be supported by substantial government control of the economy actually hurt the state industries and corporations as much as they did the private ones. Many government-controlled industries found themselves close to bankruptcy and were forced to turn to the Central Bank for loans in order to remain solvent. The Central Bank, bypassing normal budgeting procedures, lent enormous sums of money to nationalized industries as well as other government agencies. This proved to be an important factor in spurring increases in currency emissions, as table 24 shows, in turn further fueling inflationary pressures. During the fiscal year 1971–72 the government deficit rose from 10 to 26 billion escudos.

It is important to stress that the growing pattern of agencies turning toward the Central Bank in order to make ends meet had serious political as well as economic effects. It contributed to the government's loss of control and centralized authority over the general financial structure, thereby making it more difficult to reverse policies. The Office of the Budget and the Ministry of Finance found it increasingly difficult to coordinate the budget of the state sector and keep tabs on the vast state apparatus. During the Allende years the Ministry of Finance lost not only the initiative over general economic policy to the Ministry of Economics under Vuskovic's direction, but substantial control over the budgetary process. In the crisis atmosphere of the Allende

Table 23. Number of Requisitions and Interventions by Time Periods, November 1970–November 1972

Period	Interventions	Requisitions	Total
November–December 1970	37	1	38
January–February 1971	23	—	23
March–April 1971	1	5	6
May–June 1971	12	12	24
July–August 1971	9	6	15
September–October 1971	24	7	31
November–December 1971	21	9	30
January–February 1972	13	6	19
March–April 1972	14	7	21
May–June 1972	16	3	19
July–August 1972	7	18	25
September–October 1972[a]	23	48	71
November 1972	2	4	6
Total	202	126	328

SOURCE: Based on Instituto de Economía, *La economía chilena en 1972*, pp. 116 ff; cited in Stefan de Vylder, *Allende's Chile: The Political Economy at the Rise and Fall of the Unidad Popular* (Cambridge: Cambridge University Press, 1976), p. 146.

[a] During the "October events" a large number of enterprises were subjected to intervention or requisition for participation in the general lockout. Most of these companies were later returned to their owners.

years, the already cumbersome and decentralized Chilean public sector became more and more unmanageable. The bold effort to gain control of essential sectors of the economy did not help to counteract the ill effects of the early expansionist policies but only created more difficulties which further precluded extrication.

At the root of the difficulties in economic policy and state management were more basic political problems which can be traced to the coalition nature of a government operating within the rules of traditional Chilean politics. The Popular Unity parties were intent not only on bringing about change in Chilean society, often in different directions, but on maximizing their own party fortunes, according to the precepts of traditional Chilean party politics. Despite the parties' recourse to demonstrations and occasional violence, in the final analysis their "power capability" was measured by electoral success. This continued to be paramount in Chilean politics, and indirectly all groups, including the MIR, would turn to the ballot box and concern themselves with patronage and electoral considerations. This made it very difficult to impose any kind of centralized control over, or clear direction on, the government program. Not only did the president have to spend an enormous amount of time dealing with strikes and disputes by public employees and private unions and associations, he also had to contend with orchestrating an enormously complex coalition government.

From the outset the Popular Unity parties implemented a complex quota system to give each party organization access to a wealth of government patronage. From the level of ministers down through the undersecretaries to

Table 24. Increases in Money Supply and in Prices, December 1970 to July 1973 (in percentages)

Period	Percentage Increase in Money Supply	Percentage Increase in Prices
December 1970–December 1971	110.5	22.1
December 1971–December 1972	164.9	163.4
January 1972–January 1973	190.5	180.3
February 1972–February 1973	198.2	174.1
March 1972–March 1973	198.2	183.3
April 1972–April 1973	210.9	195.5
May 1972–May 1973	230.2	238.5
June 1972–June 1973	257.4	283.4
July 1972–July 1973	286.7	323.6

SOURCE: *El Mercurio,* 26 August 1973.

the lowest officials in the public bureaucracy, elaborate schemes were instituted to divide up public employment and responsibility. By and large the quota system was determined by the electoral strength of each political party. Conflicts and disputes were common. For example, when the *intendente* of Valparaiso resigned, the Radicals feared they would be denied the post, which they felt was theirs. They were particularly concerned since they had lost considerable ground in the municipal election of 1971. After much frustrating debate, Allende opted for appointing a "neutral" military officer to the post—a harbinger of things to come.

Cleavages also arose in government agencies. Not only the weight of bureaucratic practices but party cleavages cut down on the effectiveness of agency actions in implementing change. For example, the Socialist vice-president of INDAP, one of the key organizations of the agrarian reform movement, was attacked publicly by leaders of the Movement of Popular United Action (MAPU) in a power play that shook the organization.[36] Coalition difficulties were compounded by the further fractionalization of the parties of the Center, who were clearly caught in the centrifugal tendencies of Chilean politics. After the municipal elections the Radical party split, with a sizable faction arguing that the party leadership was too close to the Marxist position. Though the PIR remained temporarily in the government coalition, it was a new political entity to be reckoned with. The MAPU also split when a fragment of the Christian Democratic party broke away and formed the *Izquierda Cristiana*. Fractionalization made the complex task of allocating patronage to different elements of the coalition even more time-consuming. Allende argued that "there are more forces now supporting the government... but its base has been weakened by the internal problems of the parties."[37] In spite of his calls for the creation of a single party out of the Popular Unity coalition, the tradition of "going it alone" proved too strong.

The problems of patronage and quotas became even more demanding with the takeover of industries. The *interventores* (receivers) were appointed, particularly in later stages, largely as a reward for party activity and to insure that particular parties and factions had industries "of their own." Many interventores were very competent and dedicated. Others became notorious for their lack of knowledge of the industry they were supposed to regulate and for the element of political corruption that they introduced. In March 1972 the Communist party issued a strong criticism of the interventores, noting that they often simply replaced the old managers, living in the same houses and driving the same cars. It called for a clear and concise plan for the development of the country.[38]

Finally, the politics of quotas and political appointments led to a significant loss of authority in government agencies as well as state operated industries. Workers simply would not take orders from managers who belonged to other parties.[39] Often the simplest decisions in factories had to be resolved by party meetings or orders from party authorities on the outside. In the early years of the Allende administration perhaps the most significant example of this problem took place in the copper mines when Communist managers were appointed. Unions under the direction of the Popular Socialist party, a leftist party not in the coalition, took strong issue with the direction provided by the Communist managers. The party released the following statement in January 1972.

The USOPO believes, and makes it public, that the Communist party, when it comes to Chuquicamata, must change its attitude in its treatment of the workers....We have seen that it is its clear intent to exercise party predominance at all costs, without hesitating as to the means employed and the consequences which might result to the interests of the workers and the economy of the country.[40]

The political competition and quota system thus not only cut down on the efficiency of the government and led to serious political divisions and conflicts, but it also reinforced the decentralized and autonomous tendencies of much of the Chilean state, making it more difficult for those in the top policy-making positions to impose authority and chart the general direction of the government.

While this study has stressed the importance of patronage and electoral considerations in accounting for much of the difficulty of coordination and management, it would be a serious mistake to ignore the profound ideological disagreements and differences wihin the coalition. Both elements interacted, contributing not only to the lack of direction of the governmental effort but to its failure to respond in a unified and forceful way when decisive action was called for. In fact ideological disagreements often meant that sectors within the Popular Unity government worked at cross-purposes with one another. The Socialists stressed mobilization and worker participation, while the Communists argued for a slower course of action aimed at consolidating gains in the control of the productive sectors of the economy. Some elements of the

Socialist party and minor parties such as the MAPU pressed for radical mobilization and forced expropriation, stressing the need to prepare for armed conflict. The Left knew that it had to act together if any progress was to be made, but serious policy differences undermined concerted action.[41]

Particularly after the negative consequences of early policies became apparent, both the president and the Communist party became increasingly critical of the strategy of taking over the economy as fast as possible. Clear strains became public in December 1971 when some parties of the Popular Unity coalition, supporting a by-election candidate, issued a platform statement calling for nonpayment of landowners for expropriated lands. The Communist party condemned this statement in very strong terms.

One of the most serious evidences of a clear split in the parties came in the city of Concepción in the fall of 1972 when regional members of the Popular Unity coalition, in alliance with the MIR, sought forcibly to prevent an authorized demonstration by opposition elements. They argued that such marches gave comfort to Fascist elements and undermined the Popular Unity government. In the ensuing struggle, the police were forced to intervene, and one student, a member of an extreme leftist group, was killed.

The reaction to the death of the student and the confrontation in Concepción was immediate and widespread. With the exception of the Communist party, the regional organizations of the governing coalition called for an immediate dismissal of the intendente of the province, a Communist, and the dissolution of the police antiriot unit. Demonstrators in the capital expressed their anger by yelling slogans such as "Reformism opens the door to fascism" and "Down with politics of conciliation." The regional organization of the coalition issued a statement in which it argued that the events of Concepción showed that there were two currents among the people:

One [group] believes that it is possible to get along with the enemies of the people, which in practice means forgetting the existence of a class struggle, which seeks to rely on the apparatus of the State and not on the power of the people and the masses and even seeks a repression of those sectors of the left which don't share their policy of conciliation . . . .

The other policy affirms the conviction that it is not possible to conciliate with the enemies of the working class. It holds that the contradictions between exploiters and exploited remain and are becoming more intense. It holds that it is necessary to rely on the forced and organized mobilization of the masses, rejecting all dogmatism and sectarianism in the bosom of the people . . . . This policy rejects the tendency to assign in fact a neutral posture to the popular Government and requires that the force of the Government be joined with the force of the people to spur and channel the Chilean revolution.[42]

The Communist party, in a press conference held by its secretary general, strongly condemned the events in Concepción and argued that the other parties of the Popular Unity and the MIR had taken "an erroneous path." He added:

Let it be clear that we are in favor of recognizing the rights of the opposition when it is manifested through legal channels. . . . We believe that there is no possibility today, in the current moment, to modify that legality, that institutional structure, by any means, neither through legal means nor through extralegal means. . . . We feel that there is urgency in closing the ranks around the program of the UP, the government of the UP and the President of the Republic, and that it is possible to have a correlation of forces since it is not true that those who are not with the government are fascists. . . . To be a revolutionary is not to take over things because that is easy when one knows that the government will not repress you. To be a revolutionary is to win the battle of production . . . unfortunately not everyone agrees with this.[43]

This debate clearly illustrates the dilemma faced by Allende and the more Center-oriented elements of the coalition. Because of electoral and patronage obligations and because of significant disagreements as to the course of action, Allende had little control over the actions of many officials and parties within the government. A superb politician, he was adept at resolving the day-to-day disputes which arose, but he was unable to steer a clear course, either one which provoked a clear and rapid confrontation, which he argued against, or one of moderation, which he advocated but could not consistently follow. As a master of the art of the possible, Allende was being driven further and further into an impossible situation. Radomiro Tomic expressed Allende's dilemma clearly in August 1971 when he said, "The UP finds itself obligated to live on daily expediencies at the service of limited objectives, which are the only ones within its reach. . . ."[44] Ironically, had the matter merely been one of different ideological perspectives, it might have been possible to reach accommodation and set new directions (as the coalition tried more or less successfully to do in several famous "self-criticism" sessions). But the political problem involved more than overall strategy. It also involved the more mundane politics of a disparate coalition, and as will be noted below, it involved a cyclical and escalating confrontation with the opposition which further reduced possible options.

As time went on the problem of violence became increasingly important. Yet it, along with the mounting difficulties in the economy, was a basically unsolvable problem for Allende. He could cajole and try to persuade, as he did in an open meeting in Concepción and in a face-to-face debate with the MIR, but he could not repress the revolutionary Left and those sectors within the coalition bent on spontaneous acts. Allende had too much respect for the symbols of the Cuban Revolution and the guerrilla struggles elsewhere in Latin America to be identified as a betrayer of a "revolutionary" cause.[45] In 1969 a few *pobladores* had been killed in a confrontation with the police and it became an immediate national disaster, with the minister of the interior and President Frei himself held responsible for the massacre. A president of the people could simply not risk such a confrontation—particularly in view of the past political significance of such tragedies. Indeed, when a poblador was killed by the police, Allende went in person and virtually alone to apologize for the incident. The position of the government on this matter was repeatedly stressed by the head of the Communist party in his critique of the Left: "Neither the President of the Republic, Salvador Allende, nor the parties of the UP and in the first place the Communist party, believe, even remotely, that repressive measures can be taken against groups of workers, farmers, and students who violate the law. The MIR knows this well and takes advantage of it."[46] Yet leftist violence was often simply a response to rightist violence, which, toward the end of the Allende years, would eventually overshadow leftist violence in an increasingly ominous vicious circle of action and reaction.

That violence itself would become an important issue on its own right is dramatically illustrated by a poll taken in August 1972. As table 25 indicates, 83 percent of Chileans agreed that the country was living in a climate of violence. Though 98 percent of the highest socioeconomic group concurred with that judgment, it was shared by 75 percent of the nation's lowest socioeconomic group. What is even more important, however, is the distribution of blame for violence. Table 26 shows that Chileans blamed both sides, the government as well as the opposition, for encouraging violence. Predictably, the highest socioeconomic group placed the blame primarily on the government, while the lowest socioeconomic group blamed the opposition. What is most significant, however, is that a majority of individuals thought that the government was either primarily responsible for the violence or shared the responsibility for it. Even 18 percent of the lowest socioeconomic category believed that the government was at least partially to blame for the climate of disorder. This clearly posed a severe problem for the legitimacy of authority in Chile. Not only was the government viewed as being unable to control violence, but a significant portion of the population believed that it was responsible for violence. As Juan Linz notes, the problem of order is one of the most vexing ones for a democratic regime. It is even more vexing for a

Table 25. Responses to the Survey Question, "At This Time in Chile, Do You Think That There Is a Climate of Violence?"

	SOCIOECONOMIC GROUPS			
	Upper	Middle	Lower	Total
Yes	98%	92%	75%	83%
No	2	8	25	17

SOURCE: *Ercilla*, 13–19 September 1972, p. 11.

Table 26. Responses to the Survey Question, "If You Think That There Is a Climate of Violence in Chile at This Time, Do You Think That It is Encouraged by the Government or the Opposition?"

| | SOCIOECONOMIC GROUPS | | | |
	Upper	Middle	Lower	Total
Government	36%	27%	18%	23%
Opposition	7	20	35	27
Other sectors	54	44	22	33
No climate of violence	2	8	25	17

SOURCE: *Ercilla*, 13–19 September 1972, p. 11.

democratic regime attempting to carry out significant transformations of society with a diverse and disorganized coalition and a multiplicity of institutional political constraints in a climate of growing economic difficulty.[47]

The Opposition

Political and economic problems of the government were compounded by serious difficulties with the opposition. The process was dialectical: objections of the oppostion were due in part to government policies and government policies were due in part to the reactions of the opposition. Hoarding and sabotage in certain industries, both national and foreign, worsened the situation and forced the government to take a stronger and more aggressive stand. Foreign funds were used in a massive propaganda barrage aimed at discrediting the government through the right-wing press. Every incident of violence, every confrontation, every negative economic item was magnified, further polarizing the political atmosphere and undermining the economy.

The National party had opposed governmental initiatives from the outset, when its congressmen refused to vote for Allende's election. The only exception of importance was the unanimous vote in favor of the government's constitutional amendment nationalizing the copper mines. In addition, the ultra-right *Patria y Libertad* did not hesitate to engage in violent harrassment.[48] What was crucial, however, was the role of the Christian Democratic party. As the key centrist party the Christian Democrats had made Allende's election possible, and their continued support was needed lest the government run afoul of the Congress. As noted earlier, this understanding did break down as the Christian Democrats sponsored resolutions on areas of the economy, passed by the Congress, as a direct challenge to the president.

The tenuous Christian Democratic agreement with the government worked out around the Statute of Guarantees had actually begun to erode some months earlier. In July 1971 an agreement between the government and the Christian Democrats, through which the latter would control the leadership of the Senate while the Popular Unity coalition would control the Chamber of Deputies, broke down. At the same time the Christian Democrats joined the National Party in running an opposition candidate against the government in a by-election, voted against the government plan for a unicameral legislature, and finally, after three earlier refusals, joined the Nationals in the impeachment of José Toha, the minister of the interior. The loss of the Christian Democrats in Congress would pave the way for a series of impeachment attempts and maneuvers between the executive and the Congress that would sorely try the institutional stability of the country. Economic and fiscal difficulties would be compounded by the refusal of the legislature to consider new taxes to meet governmental deficits.

The difficulty was that, like Allende, the left-wing faction of the Christian Democratic party was subject to pressure not only from the right-wing faction of the party but from other parties.[49] Pressures were not only ideological but narrowly political in origin, stemming from the requirements of electoral survival in a competitive party system. Though many Christian Democrats shared the broad goals of the Allende administration, as members and leaders of an opposition party they had different stakes and interests. Above all, they needed to protect the autonomy and integrity of their party and see to it that it maintained its strength, defined primarily in terms of electoral success. As a centrist party, the Christian Democrats were particularly aware of the potential for erosion of support from either side. As party interests took on added importance, the progressive wing of the party began to lose its controlling influence in party affairs. Two factors were contributory in enhancing the importance of narrow party stakes for the leadership and the position of the more conservative elements. In the first place, the disorder and violence accompanying the early changes had had a significant impact on the party. Rural violence and the takeover of industries had created an atmosphere of uncertainty further (and ably) exaggerated by the right-wing press. Of particular significance was the assassination of Edmundo Perez Zujovic, a close friend of President Frei and a former minister of the interior, who had been widely attacked and accused of the "murder" of the pobladores of Puerto Montt. Though Allende immediately condemned the assassination, many Christian Democrats felt that the media, much of which was affiliated with government parties, had great responsibility for intensifying the public attacks on Perez and other members of the party. Furthermore, elements in the party connected with Chile's private economic sector had reacted with horror at the government's attempts to take over industrial, commercial, and financial institutions. As early as September 1971, the moderate Christian Democratic senator Renán Fuentealba suggested that the government might be violating the Statute of Guarantees. He specifically mentioned attacks on key figures of his party in the government press, attempts to curb the Christian Democratic media, and incidents of uncontrolled urban violence.[50]

Concern over uncontrolled violence, attacks by the press, and the speed with which the government was pushing its program were not, however, the only issues that affected the position of the Christian Democrats and undermined the leverage of the progressives or moderates. Just as important was the dilemma of survival for an electoral party of the Center in a highly polarized context. The April 1971 municipal elections were thus an important turning point. In those elections the government did very well, while the Christian Democrats continued to lose their share of the electorate. Under such circumstances any accommodation policy with the government appeared to be politically risky.

The gravity of these political problems came to the fore in a by-election for a congressional seat on 18 July 1971. Since only one seat could be filled, the contest would of necessity be a zero-sum game in which only one candidate could win. If both the National party and the Christian Democrats put up a candidate against the Popular Unity coalition, the latter stood a good chance of winning as it had in the presidential election. Strong pressure came to bear, both inside and outside of the Christian Democratic party, for the formation of a coalition to prevent a government victory.

In these difficult circumstances, and at the initiative of youthful elements of the party, Christian Democrats proposed to Allende that an agreement be worked out to prevent a race that would further polarize Chilean politics. According to the proposal, the government would recognize that the seat should be a Christian Democratic seat, since it had been held earlier by a Christian Democrat, and would present no candidate. The Christian Democrats, in turn, would run a candidate acceptable to the president and abide by the same principle in future by-elections.

The proposal, however, never got off the ground, mainly because of opposition from the Socialist party. Failure to avoid a polarized race led to a joint candidacy between the Christian Democrats and the Nationals and to a political alliance which would survive through the Allende years.[51] In the bitter race which followed, the opposition candidate won. The race clearly added to the polarization of Chilean politics, not only because of its high visibility and the barrage of attacks and counterattacks but also because the opposition alliance led to a split in the ranks of the Christian Democrats. The formation of the Christian Left, which pledged support to the government, further undermined the viability of the Christian Democrats as a viable Center option by adding to the strength of the party's right wing. Elements on both sides of the political spectrum closest to the Center, who had been instrumental in structuring the agreement which made the Allende presidency possible, were abandoning their coalitions. As fragments of the established parties, they were heading for political oblivion, with little role to play in a more rigid and confrontational politics.

The Failure of Centrist Compromise

The increased polarization and loss of support from Christian Democratic circles eventually led to the adoption, in a joint session of Congress on 20 February 1972, of a constitutional amendment, designed to regulate the government's role in the economy. For the first time in decades, Chile faced a serious constitutional crisis threatening the survival of the regime.

In narrowly legal terms, confrontation between government and opposition resulted from the opposition's claim that the president could not veto the proposed reforms and that the only way out of an impasse, short of presidential capitulation, was the submission of the measure to a national plebiscite. Allende, in turn, argued that he indeed could veto the constitutional legislation and that his item vetoes would stand unless rejected by a two-thirds vote of the Congress. Allende insisted that a constitutional amendment required the same stringent procedures called for in the adoption of a simple law. The opposition maintained that the 1970 constitutional reforms established the procedure of a plebiscite precisely in order to resolve an impasse between the president and a majority of Congress. In this highly formalized system, where very specific legal clauses were of the utmost importance, the reforms lent themselves to differing interpretations of the fundamental law of the land.[52] Underlying the dispute were certain political realities. The congressional role had been strongly reduced in Chilean politics. The Christian Democrats, who had supported such a reduction, had hoped that they would still be in the presidency. Ironically, they were now the largest single party in a legislature whose only powers were negative ones. It could reject or approve, but no longer could it bargain and compromise. The arena of accommodation had disappeared, and to counteract a president intent on pursuing his program it was necessary to have enough votes to override a veto. The congressional opposition was short of two-thirds majority, and Allende clearly had the upper hand. With the power of the presidency it was possible to institute major governmental initiatives without legislative concurrence. And yet Allende and his advisers realized that he could probably not win a plebiscite involving a simple yes or no answer on a basic issue if a plebiscite were forced. The president's early confidence that a majority of the people would support his position had disappeared.

On two separate occasions in 1972, direct talks were opened between the Christian Democrats and government officials in an attempt to resolve the impasse over the constitutional amendment. Centrists on both sides noted that the reforms adopted by Congress incorporated some ideas congruent with the Popular Unity platform. But it was not only ideological questions that had to be resolved: practical political questions were also at stake. The government did not want the opposition dictating the terms for each nationalization; the

Christian Democrats were fearful that if too many nationalized industries fell into the hands of government parties, their political position would be severely undermined.

The first set of talks, in March 1972, entrusted by Allende to the centrist Partido de Izquierda Radical, ran into immediate difficulties after the minister of economy, who was skeptical of the compromise attempt, set out forcibly to expropriate major industries designated by the government for the social sector. The PIR and the Radical party objected, claiming that the action had not been sanctioned by the parties in the government coalition. The minister, Pedro Vuskovic, with the backing of other sectors of the government, notably the Socialists, was trying to present the bargainers with a *fait accompli*. The Vuskovic actions and Socialist opposition led to the cancellation of the talks in early April. Pressure from the Left also contributed to the erosion of the government's Center position as the PIR decided to resign from the cabinet and join the opposition, arguing that the government was not serious about wanting to avoid a clash between constitutional powers. Their action further undermined the chances for success of future compromise attempts. The departure of the PIR severely challenged the government's oft-repeated contention that the Popular Unity was a broad coalition including non-Marxist middle sectors and meant the loss of a group which included respected political leaders such as Senators Luis Bossay and Alberto Baltra. Allende, unwilling to break with his own Socialist party, interpreted the exit of the PIR as a personal betrayal and accepted its ministers' resignations "with pleasure."[53] While the Socialists noted that the PIR had been a representative of the ruling class all along, the Communist party expressed deep regret at the erosion of government support. Just as the decision to ally with the Nationals had stripped the Christian Democrats of elements on its Left, so the attempts to compromise contributed to a further erosion of a center posture, this time from the right wing of the government. The possibility of a centrist consensus was being rendered even more difficult by the tendency of Chile's centrifugal forces to fragment the Center. The fragmentation of the Center had now become a cause as well as a symptom of profound crisis.

The breakdown of the talks was followed in the next few weeks by enormous mass demonstrations in the streets of Santiago organized by government and opposition, strikes by doctors, an accusation by the MIR that the military was planning a coup, strikes in the copper mines, and a tense election for rector of the University of Chile in which the government candidate lost by a substantial margin.

In early June, in this atmosphere of political conflict, amid a deteriorating economic situation, the Popular Unity parties met for another round of "self criticism." Allende, with support primarily from the Communist party, sought to stem the tide of anarchy by attempting a change in direction. He relieved Vuskovik of his central role in economic policy-making and named Orlando Millas, a leading Communist intellectual, to the important post of minister of finance. The government also called for renewed efforts to reach an accommodation with the Christian Democrats over the smoldering constitutional impasse. Secret talks, later made public, were initiated in June 1972, with the minister of justice, a Radical, representing the government. Millas, for one, noted that "it would be deadly to continue to widen the group of enemies and, to the contrary, it will be necessary to make concessions, and at least neutralize certain social sectors and groups by remedying tactical mistakes."[54] However, once again the position of the Communist party was not fully supported by the Socialist party, whose leadership gave reluctant approval to the talks. Vuskovic expressed Socialist sentiment when he said: "It is not possible to consolidate what has been done so far when the enemies of the workers maintain important bases of support. To complete the social area is a requisite not only to advance to socialism, but also to defend what has been accomplished."[55]

On the side of the opposition, centrist elements once again signaled the need to reach an accommodation. Senator Fuentealba of the PDC stated:

Aside from the legal conflict, there exists the danger of confrontation which can result from the legal conflict. Open fighting will come if this continues and no agreements are reached; fighting in the streets, fight for power, concentrations, manifestations, forums . . . . A period of agitation will result whose consequences may be very grave for the tranquility of the country and the normal development of our democratic processes.[56]

But Fuentealba and his colleagues were strongly attacked by the Right for not being aware of the "Communist threat,"[57] and the General Confederation of Production and Commerce, representing large economic interests, issued a statement "expressing concern that the experience so far makes it necessary, unfortunately, to view with skepticism this new dialogue, at the congressional level, without the participation of the private sector organizations [gremios]."[58]

Considerable progress was made in the talks and a basic agreement in principle was worked out. It involved seven main points:

1. The transfer to the state sector or a mixed sector of approximately eighty of the most strategic industries, both foreign and domestic. The agreement included norms for compensation.

2. A requirement that in future a specific law of Congress would be required to pass industries into the state or mixed sectors.

3. Restrictions on the executive's ability to intervene on a temporary basis in private firms.

4. Specific norms for worker participation in the administration of mixed

enterprises, especially banks, several of which would remain in the hands of a majority of their workers.

    5. Creation of worker-managed enterprises.

    6. Creation of a judicial body to decide complaints of discriminatory treatment of enterprises not in the state sector.

    7. Allocation of a substantial portion of public funds for publicity to newspapers, radio, and television stations in private hands.[59]

The agreement was long and complex, and involved significant concessions on both sides, but particularly on the side of the president. It allowed for the possibility of worker-controlled industries not tied in with a state network and restricted the future ability of the president to bring private enterprises into the public sphere. It committed the president to a subsidy of the opposition press with state funds. Some matters were not resolved, including the difficult issue of whether the paper monopoly would be allowed into the public sector, which would have given the government potential control over the availability of newsprint. Nevertheless, fundamental issues were settled. These issues were at the core of the primary disputes between the government and the largest opposition party and their resolution would have helped to defuse much of the confrontation. Even if elements on both extremes, Right and Left, had balked, an agreement by the Center could have gone a long way toward consolidating a process of change, albeit more gradual.

    And yet, despite the fact that the leadership of the Christian Democrats supported the compromise, compromise was blocked by the refusal of the more conservative faction of the party to go along. Ignoring the pleas of Agustín Gumucio, an ex-Christian Democrat now serving as a government negotiator who said that "we think that we could reach an agreement on pending matters if we only had some additional time . . . . We have worked in a climate of mutual respect...," the conservative faction of the party forced an immediate vote in the Senate which ended all compromise efforts.[60] This faction was concerned about the ambivalent posture of the party. While the talks were going on, the Christian Democrats were not only engaged with other opposition parties in another bitter by-election against a government candidate but they also had approved an impeachment accusation against the minister of the interior. The electoral dangers of an ambivalent posture were underscored by a third event. The Christian Democrats had presented their own candidate for the student federation of the University of Chile, refusing to join the Nationals; as a result the Communist party candidate won. The Conservative faction was determined not to concede anything. It had a high regard for the president's considerable political skills and a low regard for his trustworthiness and felt that in the conversations the leadership had been outmaneuvered by a more experienced politician. They argued that Allende could be dealt with only from a position of unquestioned strength.[61] Though the progressive elements had majority support in the party, they were unable and unwilling to force the issue. As a group the Christian Democrats showed their reluctance to take risks and strike out on a clear middle course. The irony is that elements on Allende's left also felt that the government should not bargain with the opposition except from a position of unquestioned strength. The presence on both sides of sectors arguing for higher bargaining demands confused and clouded the perceptions of moderates on the one side and the preferences of the moderate actors on the other, and often contributed to rendering the positions of the actors in the Center hesitant and ambivalent.

By the middle of July 1972, centrist agreement still proved elusive. Though Allende had attempted a policy change, it had been slow in coming, and the Christian Democrats were not prepared to bargain. Above all, they wanted to maximize their goal of electoral viability in the hopes of recapturing the presidency in 1976. The rightist Christian Democrats were confident that they had an upper hand. The government could not win a plebiscite and was unwilling to risk one. They hoped that economic hardship, anarchy, and instability would favor them in the approaching 1973 congressional elections. Why compromise, given all the difficulties and uncertainties of compromise under such circumstances?

At a critical turning point, the lonely voices in the government and the opposition calling for accommodation went unheeded. There was little concern that a crisis of regime might not only lead to the destruction of any hope for a Socialist revolution, but might destroy the very democratic rules of the game. Chileans were generally convinced that they were different—that in spite of all their difficulties they were not like other Latin Americans—and that a breakdown of regime was simply out of the question. Narrow stakes—group stakes—prevailed. As a result, the politics of mobilization and confrontation were exacerbated as everyone looked forward to the March 1973 congressional elections as a way out of the deadlock.

The Politics of Mobilization and Confrontation

When the Popular Unity government was inaugurated, mass marches and rallies, typical of a presidential campaign, did not taper off. They became a vital part of the Chilean political landscape. The government as well as the opposition turned to the mobilization of large crowds, in stadiums and in the streets, in an attempt to demonstrate their power. Thus, after the march of the empty pots in December of 1971, the Popular Unity coalition answered with a mass rally of its own. In cities across the country marches staged by one group were followed by counter-marches by another, as each side tried to prove that true popular support rested with them. When asked whether he thought that mass demonstrations, leading at times to civil disobedience, would allow for the construction of socialism, Luis Corvalán, secretary general of the Communist party, answered:

I think so, provided that our forces are superior, that the presence in the street of masses that on our side is greater than the adversaries', as has been the case up to now. For every time that they have taken the initiative, and have gone out into the streets, we have responded with demonstrations that are much stronger; and this has forced them to retreat.[62]

The failure to compromise in July 1972, however, led to a fundamental and qualitative change in this game of political mobilization. No longer would it be a matter of increasing bargaining stakes by filling more corners of the Plaza Bulnes or more seats in the national stadium. The clear message of the aborted negotiations—that resolution to the Chilean crisis could only come from winning or losing decisively in the 1973 congressional elections eight months later—led to an unprecedented effort by a multitude of political actors to prove *actual* as opposed to *potential* power capability.[63] Political mobilization became political confrontation. As early as August 1972 a rash of confrontations took place between the government and its supporters and groups on both the Left and the Right. These confrontations would continue to escalate to such a point that the country would grind to a halt in October of that year. A feeling of crisis and fear would grip the country. For the first time Chileans talked seriously of civil war.

One of the most important features of the new confrontation was the direct involvement for the first time on a massive scale of the *gremios,* representing thousands of small business associations. On 22 August retail merchants declared a one-day national strike, and in early September the truckers went out on a strike.[64] Acting out of fear of economic threats occasioned both by the faltering economy and government attempts to ration distribution of supplies and regulate transportation, they moved to defend their basic economic interests. Because of the importance of the trucking industry in the Chilean economy, the truckers' strike in particular dealt a serious blow to the government and served to rally other groups and associations who subsequently joined the movement to paralyze the economy. What is important about this movement is that it marked a change from party-directed and party-manipulated mobilization to direct mobilization by both big and small businessmen seeking to protect their stakes in the system. Christian Democratic elements, as well as sectors of the National party who had a role in the organization of these groups in the late 1960s, found that they acted increasingly on their own, often at cross-purposes with party leadership. Their independence in turn aggravated the problem of competition between the Christian Democrats and the Nationals, further forcing the Christian Democrats to harden their position lest they lose their perceived support among large sectors of the middle class.[65] Spokesmen for both parties rushed to express solidarity with the myriad striking groups.

The government and parties of the Left moved swiftly to counteract the effects of the mobilization of the petite bourgeoisie. The *Juntas de Abastecimientos y Precios* (JAPs), originally set up to channel goods and food to poorer neighborhoods, were extended to create a vast, government-run network to ration supplies. The government, with the cooperation of the Central Labor Federation (CUT), sought to keep industries open and functioning, and enlisted the support of students, workers, and professionals sympathetic to the government coalition in counter-strikes. But the actions of the opposition also gave renewed impetus to more revolutionary elements both in the Popular-Unity coalition and outside it, who moved to set up *comandos comunales*, *comandos campesinos*, and *cordones industriales* with paramilitary characterisitics to defend communities, farms, and factories. Like the gremios, these organizations acted on the fringes of the established leadership of political parties, forming the base of a small, though increasingly radicalized sector of the working class. Their actions would have political consequences similar to those resulting from the actions of the gremios. They would drive a further wedge in the unity of the Popular Unity coalition and put great pressure on established parties increasingly to radicalize the process of transformation.[66] Ironically, it was the counter-mobilization of the petite bourgoisie responding to real, contrived, and imaginary threats which finally engendered, in dialectical fashion, a significant and autonomous mobilization of the working class. Aside from a few scattered initiatives by groups such as the MIR, prior to October 1972 the established government parties had maintained political control over their followers and the bulk of Chile's workers. It took the massive onslaught of the *huelgas patronales* to begin to consolidate a degree of class consciousness and autonomous action. Even so, throughout the Allende period radicalized sectors of the working class remained a minority, and the most significant destabilizing and uncontrolled mobilization would continue to be the counter-mobilization of the middle class. The breakdown of Chilean democracy was more the result of counter-mobilization against perceived threats than excessive mobilization of sectors demanding their due.[67]

As it had from the very beginning, the mass media played a key role in this period of escalating confrontation. The media, which saturated every corner of the small country, became the principal exponent of the most extreme views. It was hard to separate the real battle from the symbolic battle of the newspapers, radio, and television screens. Events were exaggerated and distorted. Lies and character assassination were the order of the day. Everything took on political significance, and even the most insignificant event became a crucial and more ominous turning point. Opposition papers, and in particular the influencial *El Mercurio*, which had received large sums of money from U.S. intelligence, were particularly skillful in rallying the vast array of opposition groups and organizations. For the most part the wielders of information acted independently of the political leadership, and their strident accusations and counter-accusations contributed to further polarization in the already volatile atmosphere. With the erosion of regular bargaining channels, leaders on each side were forced to rely more and more on a medium which did not always convey with accuracy the positions of leaders on the other side. Symbolic politics increasingly replaced "real" politics, further undermining the possiblity of creating institutionalized channels for accommodation. Leaders of the Popular Unity government and of the Christian Democrats both expressed their despair at the excesses of their respective media organizations, some going so far as to say that the media was now the tail wagging the national dog.[68]

It soon became clear that confrontation politics had moved the fulcrum of the Chilean political system outside the realms of traditional decision-making institutions. The political leadership had lost, in large measure, control over its own followers. Political elites on both sides had resorted to the politics of mobilization and manipulation of the media in an effort to strengthen their own position vis-à-vis the opposition. As long as the leadership of both sides had continued to work through established institutional mechanisms of accommodation, mobilizational politics remained a tool of the leadership. However, as soon as accommodationist mechanisms faltered—as soon as the most salient and serious crisis of Chilean politics could no longer be resolved through the structuring of a Center consensus—mobilizational politics took on a life of its own. Political elites who strove for maximum political influence found themselves losing their preeminent positions in Chilean politics. For the government the matter was even more serious; not only did it have less and less influence over the actions of its many followers on the Left, but to a large degree it had lost authority over Chilean society. The economy, already on the brink of collapse, was buffeted further. By December 1972 inflation was at a record 150 percent.[69] And once again, these developments further constrained the options for the future. The failure of the compromise attempt in mid-1972 had been a further blow to those sectors of the Popular Unity coalition who had pressed for the moderate and conciliatory approach in a secret meeting at *Lo Curro* a few weeks earlier. It was also a serious setback for the progressive sector of the Christian Democrats, which had placed its prestige and energy in the compromise attempt. The politicians had had their day. There was only one other institution which could fill the political vacuum and make it possible for the 1973 elections to take place at all. That institution was the Chilean military.

4.

The Chilean Military, the 1973 Election, and Institutional Breakdown

The failure to compromise, the resultant decline in the role of traditional mediating institutions and procedures, mobilization politics, and the steady erosion of leadership's control over its followers was accompanied by a resort to what Juan Linz calls "neutral" powers in order to resolve disputes.[1] The Contraloría, the courts, the Constitutional Tribunal, and finally the armed forces steadily became more involved in highly political and controversial disputes which clearly belonged in the legislative arena and required bargaining and compromise to achieve resolution.

The Contraloría was repeatedly asked to determine the legality of a host of government and opposition actions, including industrial and farm takeovers. Though the Contraloría's rulings at times favored the government, on many volatile questions it ruled against government actions. In August 1971, for example, it ruled against the attempts of an agency head to take over a textile firm. This case and others like it led to strong attacks on the Contraloría from the government press. The comptroller general responded in an unusual news conference by decrying the nation's polarization, which had forced an agency such as Contraloría to be either "revolutionary or reactionary."[2] Similar attacks were levied against the courts, who were also called upon to rule on the legality of controversial actions. For the most part, the conservative Chilean judiciary, faithfully interpreting existing law, did not hesitate to defend the rights of proprietorship, condemning the government's attempts to subordinate property rights to human rights and the requirements of a Socialist order. In particular, the refusal of government officials to use the police to throw invaders off private property led to serious clashes with the judicial branch.[3] The Constitutional Tribunal, in turn, was called on to rule on whether the majority in Congress or the president was right on the procedure for adopting constitutional amendments.

The involvement of these organizations in the heat of political controversy, a symptom of the failure of leaders to agree, contributed to the open politicization of previously "neutral" forces and the further deterioration of the legitimacy of the system. They came under heavy attack from the Left as representatives of bourgeois social order and were vehemently defended by the Right as the bulwarks of tradition and legality. For both sides the symbolic level had become paramount, and it became impossible to separate the rules and procedures of democracy from the institutions which in Chile embodied those rules. Thus, in the final analysis, the only "neutral" power with any real legitimacy and a capacity to mediate between contending forces was the military. But it was not until the chaotic and dangerous confrontation of October 1972, with its threat of civil war, that the armed forces intervened directly as political buffers. On 5 November, Allende brought the commander in chief of the army into his cabinet as minister of the interior. Along with military men at the head of the Ministry of Mines and the Ministry of Public Works, General Carlos Prats was charged with helping to restore order and guarantee the neutrality of the approaching congressional elections of March 1973.

When Allende took office he realized fully the importance of military neutrality if he were to carry out major aspects of his program. The government went out of its way to accommodate the armed forces' material and salary requirements.[4] Incorporation of a military man into the cabinet as minister of the interior was, however, a desperate measure of last resort that carried with it extremely grave risks. Once before, in April 1972, Allende had brought a general into the cabinet when internal disputes in the Popular Unity coalition made it difficult to name a minister of mines. That experience did not provide good precedent. The minister had complained that he lacked authority and that policy was executed according to political requirements at lower levels. He was unwilling to sign decrees of insistence in order to overrule the Contraloría, thus thwarting several government initiatives. When Allende reorganized his cabinet in June, the general did not stay on.

The incorporation of the commander in chief of the army into the cabinet could not but help to bring out latent generational, service, and political cleavages within the military institutions. It would increase tension between the elements who abhorred the Popular Unity government and were prepared to move against it with force and the "constitutionalists" who preferred not to take the enormous risks such an act would entail.

Underscoring their dependence on the military as a buffer, many leaders in both the government coalition and in the opposition went out of their way effusively to praise the military, stressing that they were basically on the military's side. However, the military was strongly criticized by a few, particularly those on the extremes of the political spectrum. Elements of the Socialist party did not hide their frustration when the military refused to sign decrees of insistence which would enable more firms to be brought into the social sector. Likewise, right-wing elements in the opposition bitterly criticized the military for initiatives aimed at stopping the wave of strikes and restoring order.[5] The officers were constrainted from both sides. On the one hand, they were not given enough authority; political cadres in the ministries continued to call the shots, as Admiral Ismael Huerta, the minister of public works, revealed with frustration. Yet the Left criticized them for blocking the Popular Unity program. On the other hand, they were criticized for legitimizing the government by an opposition banking on the government's failure to obtain a majority in the approaching congressional elections. These pressures clearly took their toll within military ranks. Particularly affected was General Carlos Prats, who made a heroic attempt to preserve the constitutional order and was accused of sympathizing with the government. (Resentment against him would surface after the March 1973 elections.) Politicians had turned to the military to resolve their problems, and in the process they had contributed to the further politicization of military institutions. When brought in to solve political problems, the military simply could not act as a "neutral" force— that is a contradiction in terms. Prats could only hope that the congressional election of 1973 would provide a solution and they could turn the whole thing back to the politicians.

The March Election: Stalemate, Renewed Confrontation, and Power Deflation

With the commanding general of the army serving as minister of the interior, the contending political forces in Chile channeled all of their energies and resources into the electoral campaign. The electoral contest would mark the culmination of the process of polarization begun years earlier, as each side joined together in structuring joint lists. Formed in July 1972, the Federation of the Popular Unity and the Democratic Confederation became concrete, tangible indicators of the total loss of any middle ground in the turbulent drama of Chilean politics. The structuring of federated parties not only indicated that each side wanted to prove it commanded majority support in the country, but it also demonstrated that individual parties on both sides feared the loss of support which they might experience at the hands of their own coalition partners. Though voters would still be able to vote for candidates identified with particular parties, lists were jointly structured, giving the voters a clear choice between mutually exclusive alternatives.[6]

For several long months the electorate was bombarded by a flurry of speeches, declarations, rallies, charges, and counter-charges of an intensity rarely seen in Chilean politics. Personal vilification became the order of the day, as the ever-present broadcast and print media sought to tarnish the images of leaders and contenders.[7] Funds from abroad and from moneyed sectors of Chilean society flowed freely into the opposition press and the campaigns of Nationals and Christian Democrats.[8]

The opposition forces argued that the election was a final and definitive plebiscite on the conduct of the Popular Unity government.[9] Both the Christian Democrats and the Nationals bitterly criticized the government's perfor-mance in the economic field and condemned what they saw as anarchy and chaos that would further damage Chilean institutions.[10] The Nationals, more than the Christian Democrats, emphasized that the struggle was a fundamental one between Marxism and democracy and that the election was merely a step in a broader and more fundamental confrontation.[11] Elements in both parties called for a concerted attempt to gain a two-thirds majority in the legislature in order to give the opposition the constitutional authority to impeach the presi-dent.[12] Further to the right, the paramilitary Patria y Libertad organization vociferously led an ever-increasing chorus of voices calling not only for a clear electoral victory but for a final solution involving armed intervention and the military defeat of the Left.[13]

The government parties were united in arguing that the Popular Unity Federation would do well in the election, but they rejected any suggestion that a parliamentary contest could be considered a plebiscite on government per-formance.[14] With the help of the military, the government sought to ensure order and to make the best of the serious economic situation. Efforts to distribute supplies and foodstuffs to the *poblaciones* were increased. How-ever, on critical issues the Left demonstrated less cohesion and unity than did the opposition. For the opposition the issue was clear—the government should be soundly defeated. For the Popular Unity coalition it was a matter not only of winning an election but of continuing to govern a country while maintain-ing a commitment to revolutionary transformations. The Communist party, and Allende himself, repeatedly called for conciliation and directed its appeal not only to elements of the working class but also to the broad middle sectors of society. The Communists often specifically called on workers of Christian Democratic persuasion to support the government. They condemned the at-mosphere of confrontation. The Communist party repeatedly spoke of the danger of civil war, adopting as its principal slogan "No—to the civil war."[15]

But a large sector of the Socialist party, including Carlos Altamirano, its executive secretary, called not for a consolidation of gains but for further acceleration of the class struggle. The Socialists interpreted the October strike as a signal of the power of the business sectors and as confirmation of their repeated arguments for a more rapid and militant mobilization of the working class. They specifically condemned the "reformism" of the Communist party as exemplified by efforts such as those of Minister Orlando Millas to resolve the still-pending question of the legalization of the public sector of the econ-omy.[16] Some Socialists went so far as to call for a resounding victory of the Popular Unity government in order to defeat tendencies within the coalition favoring "conciliation."[17] Other sectors of the Left, both in and out of the coalition, also demanded a renewed confrontation that would accelerate the "contradictions" of Chilean society and prepare the working class for a

Table 27. Comparison of the Vote Received by Opposition and Popular Unity Parties in the 1969 and 1973 Congressional Elections

Party	1969 Number of Votes	%	1973 Number of Votes	%
Popular Unity				
Socialists	294,448	12.2	678,674	18.4
Communists	383,049	15.9	595,829	16.2
IC			41,432	1.1
API			29,977	.8
MAPU			90,620	2.5
Radical	313,559	13.0	133,751	3.6
UP List			46,100	1.3
Others	65,378	2.8		
Total	1,056,434	43.9	1,616,383	43.9
Opposition				
Christian Democrats	716,547	29.8	1,049,676	28.5
National	480,523	20.0	777,084	21.1
PIR			65,120	1.8
DR			70,582	1.9
CODE ticket			33,918	.9
Total	1,197,070	49.8	1,996,380	54.2
Other				
USOPO	51,904	2.2	10,371	.3
Blank and Void	98,617	4.0	57,770	1.6
Registered	3,244,892		4,510,060	
Voting	2,406,129		3,680,307	
Abstaining	838,763	16.5	829,753	18.4

SOURCE: Electoral statistics from the Dirección del Registro Electoral.
NOTE: Party names have been abbreviated as follows:
    IC = Izquierda Cristiana
    API = Acción Popular Independiente
MAPU = Movimiento de Acción Popular Unitario
    PIR = Partido Izquierda Radical
    DR = Democracia Radical
CODE = Confederación Democrática
USOPO = Unión Socialista Popular

protracted struggle leading to fundamental revolutionary change.[18] Both the government and the opposition had in their midsts political forces seeking not only an electoral victory but further direct confrontation. Their very presence contributed to the "justification" of the arguments of the most extreme elements on both sides. It undermined further the ever more tenuous position of the moderate sectors. From both poles of Chilean politics, political prophecies became self-fulfilling prophecies.

Predictably, the March 1973 congressional elections did not resolve the political crisis. They merely illustrated further how polarized the country was

Table 28. Correlation between Vote and Occupational Category, in Santiago and Nationwide

| | Blue-collar Workers[a] | | | | Self-employed Workers[b] | | | |
| | Popular Unity | | Opposition | | Popular Unity | | Opposition | |
	Nationwide	Santiago	Nationwide	Santiago	Nationwide	Santiago	Nationwide	San
1970 presidential election	.52	.49	−.47	−.50	.13	.33	−.11	−
1971 municipal election	.46	.46	−.32	−.34	.15	.39	−.09	−
1973 congressional election	.34	.47	−.36	−.30	.08	.36	−.08	−

SOURCE: Electoral data from the Dirección del Registro Electoral; 1970 census material from the Instituto Nacional de Estadística.

NOTE: N = 287 communes.

[a]Includes artisans, miners, and industrial laborers.
[b]Includes self-employed sales and service workers.
[c]Includes professional, technical, and office employees.
[d]Includes managers and high-level administrators.

and how equally divided the contending forces were. The opposition came nowhere near achieving a two-thirds majority in the Congress, and in fact lost six deputies and two senators. The Popular Unity coalition, on the other hand, continued to be a minority coalition, receiving 43.9 percent of the votes cast to the opposition's 54.2 percent. As table 27 shows, this represented a sharp decline in the combined vote of the opposition and an increase in the vote of the Popular Unity government compared to the 1970 presidential race. However, the table also shows that, compared with the previous congressional race, the overall change was slight. In fact, with the exception of the Socialists, there was a change of only about 1 percent in the relative strength of the major parties. Only the Socialists, who no doubt inherited some of the support of the Radical party, made significant headway, gaining 6.2 percent in their relative standing. Preliminary analysis of the electoral correlates of the vote of 1973 also suggests a picture of continuity. There was no dramatic shift in the bases of support. Traditional working-class regions and sectors continued their support of the government, while the opposition continued to have strength in the countryside and more affluent areas. There seems to have been some erosion of middle sector support for the Left—with a concomitant strengthening of support in working-class and rural areas. Table 28 provides a few of these correlates, contrasting the support received by the government and the opposition over the three elections of the Popular Unity period in all of the nation's communes and in the communes of Santiago. Scattergrams reveal that the reduction of strength of the coalition among blue-collar workers suggested by the declining correlations did not take place. Rather, the coali-

| White-collar Workers [c] | | | | Managers [d] | | | | |
| Popular Unity | | Opposition | | Popular Unity | | Opposition | | |
Nationwide	Santiago	Nationwide	Santiago	Nationwide	Santiago	Nationwide	Santiago	
0	.12	−.28	−.13	−.21	−.22	−.20	.21	1970 presidential election
5	.13	−.25	−.20	.16	−.25	−.17	−.02	1971 municipal election
5	−.05	−.13	.18	.09	−.40	−.08	.47	1973 congressional election

tion seems to have increased its strength in areas with smaller concentrations of blue-collar workers.

The eagerly awaited congressional elections did not clear the political air. Instead, they gave renewed impetus to forces eager to accelerate the process of confrontation. The strong showing of the Socialist party within the Popular Unity coalition was interpreted by many as clear evidence that working-class Chileans were ready for an acceleration of the revolutionary program. By the same token, many opposition elements, concerned about the preservation of the status quo and prevailing institutions, saw the election as a signal that the rules of the game were no longer adequate to protect their goals and interests, and that unconstitutional means would have to be employed to curb the government. Violent and seditious acts escalated; military officers plotted. Important elements in the semiloyal group identified in chapter 2 moved into the disloyal category, including members of the National party and even some Christian Democrats. In this impasse Allende faced three options.

In the first place, he could have sought the continuation of a military cabinet. This would have had the obvious advantage of continuing to legitimize his minority government. The problem was that the Left in the coalition had become increasingly upset about the military presence and its dampening effect on the revolutionary program. At the same time the military officers in the cabinet were conscious of the awkward position they were in. Criticism from the Left was accompanied by strong criticism from the Right that they were serving to legitimize government policies, policies over which they often had little control.

The second strategy would have entailed a final truce with the Christian Democrats. The issue of the "areas of the economy" was the key question on the political agenda, and some kind of compromise would have had to be worked out to avoid the much-postponed final constitutional crisis. A cabinet of national unity, including Christian Democrats or prominent men with the confidence of both sides, would have been a step in this direction. This strategy was again criticized by both extremes of the political spectrum. It would have had to overcome much of the bitterness engendered by the congressional campaign. If the level of trust had been low in July 1972, the intervening months had worsened rather than improved the level of consensus.

The third strategy, one advocated by many elements within the Popular Unity, particularly on the Left, was for the government to forge ahead with renewed determination. The verdict at the polls had been encouraging—this was a good time to press ahead with the strategy of the *fait accompli*, they felt. The government had done well in maintaining popular support despite the economic crisis; if it could find new determination and direction it might increase its support and gain more victories.

Salvador Allende had great difficulty making up his mind. At first, he seriously considered the first option. His inclination was to continue a middle ground that would enable him to further implement his program with the continued support and legitimacy provided by military ministers. But it was not only the Left in the Popular Unity coalition who opposed this course: the military men themselves were simply not prepared to continue in the cabinet.[19] The experience of serving as a buffer in the highly polarized Chilean environment had taken its toll. Now that a political defeat of the government was no longer a possibility, many elements within the armed forces began to press with renewed vigor for a military solution. The constitutionalists, and particularly General Prats, were on the defensive. To avoid the harsh criticism of complicity with the government and to stave off increasing sedition in the officer corps, it was best, they felt, to allow the military to return to its professional responsibilities.

Faced with the need to form a new cabinet, Allende appointed a civilian cabinet drawn from moderate elements in the Popular Unity coalition. It was unclear whether the government planned to press for dramatic new moves or would attempt to enter a conciliatory period. At the swearing-in ceremony of the ministers, the president stressed the importance of institutional legality and pluralism. And yet, at a rally at the CUT that very evening, many of the same ministers attacked the opposition and the Christian Democrats with strong words and called for closure of the Congress.[20] Once again, the coalition and its president projected an ambivalent posture.

The Christian Democrats continued to refer to themselves as the biggest party in the country and stressed the importance of "opposition at all costs." In a meeting preparatory to the upcoming Christian Democratic Convention, Eduardo Frei noted that opposition to the government had to be categorical and total "because this position stems from an attitude of opposition to the Marxist attempt to implant totalitarianism in Chile. . . . I am being threatened by a spiritual death by Marxism and dictatorship. I don't even want to live in a Marxist country."[21]

In this tense atmosphere, the opposition was able to seize on a critical issue which once again put the government on the defensive and for the first time aligned the Catholic hierarchy openly with critics of the government. The controversy involved a government proposal, long under study, to create a Unified National Schooling System (Escuela National Unificada).[22] One of the fundamental goals contemplated in the reform was the strengthening of vocational training in the secondary school system, which was primarily designed as a preuniversity course of study.

Though the substance of the reforms was generally accepted by different sectors of the government coalition, the actual draft prepared by technical-political sectors of the Ministry of Education led to considerable government controversy.[23] Jorge Tapia Valdés, the minister of education, with backing from his Radical party, was concerned that the proposed timing of the reforms and the wording of the draft would create serious problems for the government. The reforms were to take effect in June 1973, and the draft contained highly partisan language. With the support of the president of the republic, the minister sought to delay implementation of the plan and to have a new draft proposal drawn up which could be more widely circulated for consultation before final approval. Elements of both the Socialist and Communist parties within the ministry, without adequate party consultation, pressed for the original proposal. It was that draft which came to light after the congressional elections and became the basis for a strong attack on the government's alleged goal of turning the educational system into a massive indoctrination program. Most of the original goals of the project were lost in the heated and acrimonious debate which ensued. As on previous occasions, the inability of the government to present a unified program, and the insistence of middle-level militants on rhetoric which would clearly inflame the opposition, presented the government with a serious political predicament. Not only did the church object to the proposal, which gave the opposition considerable legitimacy, but the issue served as a rallying point for opponents of the government within the armed forces.[24] All of the commanding officers of the armed services met with the beleaguered minister of education in April 1973 to protest the ENU reforms. It was clear from the meeting that they were not interested in hearing the substance of the reforms; they were primarily interested in conveying to the government that they agreed with the tone of the opposition's criticism of the entire conduct of governmental policy. The highest-ranking officers were now openly conveying their lack of neutrality on policy matters not normally in their sphere of competence or responsibility.

Clearly stung by the massive outcry against the ENU proposal, President Allende was forced to withdraw the proposal and give assurances that it would not be enacted without broad consultation. The political motivations of the opposition were further evidenced by the fact that despite the withdrawal, opposition parties continued to encourage mass demonstrations in the streets.

This incident, coming on the heels of the congressional election in which the government's performance was commendable, was extraordinarily damaging to the government. It not only provided the opposition with an issue capable of mobilizing further sectors against the government, but it also sapped the government of the momentum it needed to continue ruling the country until the 1976 presidential contest. And, to make matters worse, Allende's capitulation on the issue aggravated its already deteriorating relations with the left wing of the coalition.

In an attempt to recapture the offensive, and in a renewed attempt to show the increasingly skeptical left wing of the coalition that it had not given in, Allende's cabinet moved officially to take over forty firms which had been occupied during the October strike. This was done by a decree of insistence, with all cabinet officers signing an order to overrule the objections of the comptroller general. Predictably, that action led to immediate cries for impeachment of the entire cabinet and allegations that the government had become illegitimate.

The postelection period had once again brought a sharp renewal of the politics of confrontation. On the critical constitutional reform issue, Allende argued that the Constitutional Tribunal should and could rule on whether or not the president's position was the correct one. The inability to reach a consensus on procedural matters had led to the involvement of yet another "neutral" institution in the hope that the impossible could be arbitrated. The opposition promptly noted that the tribunal did not have jurisdiction over the matter and that it would not abide by an unfavorable decision. At the same time, the legal confrontation escalated when Congress approved another constitutional amendment to "regularize" the "reform" process by barring expropriations of rural plots under forty acres and giving titles to those who lived on the land.

Outside the halls of Congress the media escalated its rhetoric. The Communist party and the Christian Democrats traded bitter accusations after the Communist newspaper, *El Siglo*, attacked the Frei administration for receiving money from the CIA in 1964, further embittering the relations between the two groups. Renán Fuentealba, the president of the Christian Democratic party, noted that Chile was experiencing the worst totalitarian threat in its history: "The government has declared war on Chilean Democracy. War is War. We will know how to respond." Fuentealba went on to attack Allende personally for not disavowing the charges: "It was the ignoble and improper attitude of a man who says he is a man."[25]

The Christian Democratic response to the takeover of additional firms was equally bitter. Senator Patricio Aylwin, who would soon be elected to the presidency of his party in a close and heated convention, remarked that "with this decision the government of Mr. Allende has taken to extremes the almost continuous policy of doing whatever he pleases with absolute contempt for juridical norms regulating the exercise of power in a state of laws."[26] The government press countered with strong attacks criticizing opposition leaders and the Senate for "selling out."

In the midst of these charges and counter-charges a small but significant incident took place. General Carlos Prats, commander in chief of the army and former minister of the interior, spoke before a closed meeting of eight hundred officers of the Santiago garrison. His remarks, arguing for respect of the constitutional government, were met by a chorus of coughs. The "constitutionalists" within the armed forces were now clearly on the defensive.[27]

By May the government had imposed a state of emergency in Santiago, as organized groups from both sides clashed in the streets. These demonstrations came on the heels of a rash of strikes in public transportation, in the state steel mill, and in government agencies—all demanding higher wages and government guarantees against economic hardship. On top of this, miners struck at the critical El Teniente copper mine, starting a strike that would last for weeks and would force the government to cut off deliveries of copper to key customers.[28]

With the military out of the cabinet, and in an atmosphere of renewed confrontation, the government had lost its authority over the country. Displaying even greater determination than in October 1972, private economic groups of the revolutionary Left struck out on their own. The maximalists were now openly arguing for a strategy of arming the workers for the final confrontation. More than ever, the opposition parties could not keep up with the demands of their former bases and of the gremios who took most of the initiative in fighting the government.

The Supreme Court now openly criticized Allende, arguing that the country faced "a crisis of the rule of law." Police were no longer capable of controlling violence—the courts were no longer being obeyed. Allende personally exchanged a series of letters with the members of the Supreme Court, defending his government and accusing the justices of siding with order at the expense of social justice.[29] The reduction of the political arena was also evidenced by an unprecedented exchange of letters between the president and a group of retired military officers who made a public declaration deploring the effects which the economic crisis and social agitation might have on the country's national defense. Allende also went in person to engage in a bitter "dialogue" with extreme leftist employees of the Ministry of Public Works who had occupied the ministry and shut it down. When he engaged in personal conversations with striking miners in an attempt to settle the El Teniente strike, both the Socialist party and the Communist party attacked his recognition of the legitimacy of what they referred to as "opposition" workers. An increasingly lonely figure, Allende was now finding that his skilled efforts at persuasion were falling on deaf ears.

Any attempt at reopening a dialogue with the Christian Democrats, a course Allende and some of his cabinet officers urged privately and publicly, received a further setback in the third week of May when the Christian Democratic party elected a "hard line" slate to preside over the party's fortunes. In a skillfully orchestrated set of political maneuvers, former-president Frei succeeded in convincing the convention to adopt the thesis that Chile faced the prospect of a Marxist dictatorship, and that the party's response could only be one of continued and invigorated opposition. This position won by a narrow 55 percent to 45 percent margin over the thesis maintaining that Chile's problem was not too much authority, but too much anarchy. According to the progressive wing of the party, the nation's chaos could only be overcome through a policy of rapprochement and accommodation. The election of Patricio Aylwin to the presidency of the organization signaled the determination of a narrow majority to refuse to take any initiatives at finding a political solution unless the president was genuinely willing to capitulate to its demands.[30] Earlier fragmentations of the party, which had seen the left wing gradually split off, first to form the MAPU and then to form the Christian Left, had contributed to shifting the balance in favor of the party's right wing.

The election of officers from the more conservative faction had created serious structural impediments to any centrist agreement. Previously the conciliators in both the Popular Unity coalition and the Christian Democrats dominated their respective authority positions. Allende headed the government and was titular leader of his coalition; Fuentealba had represented the more progressive elements in the opposition party. Now, official attempts at an understanding between the two groups would have to be channeled through the more conservative Aylwin leadership. Any unofficial contacts with the progressive wing of the Christian Democrats would only aggravate the prospect of a settlement by raising Christian Democratic fears that any split in the party would work to the disadvantage of the fragment not identified with the official leadership, and therefore would not contribute to a political solution.[31] If a workable settlement between contending forces were to be arrived at, the Christian Democrats, through their official leadership, would have to be a party to it. The shift of power to the right would escalate the bargaining demands of the opposition and make any agreement considerably more costly to the president.[32]

Shortly after the Christian Democratic convention, the question of a compromise took on renewed urgency. In the first week of June the Constitutional Tribunal ruled that it was not competent to judge the lingering constitutional dispute between the president and Congress. The conflict was finally left without a single referee. Both sides attempted to adopt that version of the constitutional amendment which they favored, though the Contraloría ruled against the president. Congress then moved to impeach four of Allende's cabinet ministers and eight of the twenty-five provincial intendants. On 18 June the opposition Democracia Radical party issued a statement which cried, "Enough declarations—the effective fight on all fronts must begin."[33] A prominent National senator declared on nationwide television, "The president of the Republic is at present an illegitimate head of state."[34] And El Mercurio featured an article declaring:

It is the categoric duty of sensible people to put an end to looting and disorder stimulated by an inept and crazy government which smothers us. . . . In order to accomplish this task of political salvation, we have to renounce all political parties, the masquerade of elections, the poisoned and deceitful propaganda, and turn over to a few select military men the task of putting an end to political anarchy.[35]

The government responded to this upsurge of seditious talk by holding a huge mass rally to demonstrate the people's continued support for the government. It marked the beginning of the end of the Chilean "way to socialism," for a week later, on 29 June, a garrison of the Chilean military attempted a coup d'état. The coup was put down swiftly by the decisive action of General Prats. Garrisons that had hesitated were prevented from joining the revolt. But, despite the cheers from the Left, the government's "victory" proved illusory. The fate of the country was no longer merely in the hands of politicians; it had now also fallen into the hands of a divided and highly politicized military.

Efforts at Compromise: The Abdication of the Democrats

The attempted coup of 29 June 1973 marked the final turning point in the unfolding tragedy of Chilean politics. It provided President Allende with further evidence that the military could no longer be counted on as a neutral arbiter. When he called the fourteen generals of the army into his office to obtain support, only four offered categorical backing. He realized that his days as president were numbered unless he could regain political authority. He rejected the advice of the maximalist forces in his coalition who continued to press for widespread arming of workers. The president felt armed confrontation was naive and suicidal. "How many masses does one need to stop a tank?" he reportedly asked Senator Altamirano.[36] If Allende had been ambivalent before, his actions after the attempted coup clearly indicated that he was prepared to come to some kind of agreement with the Christian Democrats in a last effort to structure a compromise that would defuse the political opposition. The Christian Democrats were still the largest party in the country, and their leaders commanded great respect among vast sectors of the opposition. Even though many people were no longer interested in preserving the traditional system, a compromise between the president and the principal opposition party would have made any coup attempt, or for that matter any attempt to spark armed confrontation by the masses, extremely costly.[37]

Prominent members of the Christian Democratic party shared these sentiments and called on the party to reach an understanding with the government. Fernando Castillo, one of the most distinguished members of the progressive wing of the party and rector of the Catholic University, spoke in the name of all of the country's university presidents, saying that it was crucial that a consensus be found to defend democratic institutions. He warned, "as the danger increases, a minimum loyal consensus becomes more urgent."[38]

The situation was extraordinarily delicate. The military commanders were unwilling to join a cabinet, reflecting the unusual unrest in the ranks.[39] Since military commitment to neutrality had suffered seriously, it was Allende's hope that an agreement among politicians would help to strengthen those factions in the military who were still reluctant to violate the basic canons of traditional Chilean civil-military relations.

But compromise among the centrist forces still faced the perennial constraints of the last two and one-half years; both government and opposition faced the virulent opposition of the extreme Right and the extreme Left. Furthermore, the leadership of the Christian Democrats had shifted to the conservative side. The level of trust was at an all-time low. Group stakes and individual stakes took precedence over the stakes which most Chileans had in the ongoing system. Everyone sought to impose his own solutions; debatable issues had all but disappeared.

Efforts at compromise were immediately attacked by Altamirano, who noted:

There are those who pretend to urge "democratic dialogues" with Christian Democracy. As Socialists we say that a dialogue is possible with all those forces who clearly define themselves as against exploiters and against imperialism. We foster and will develop dialogue at the level of the masses, with all the workers, whether they are our militants or not, but we reject all dialogues with reactionary and counter-revolutionary leaderships and parties.[40]

Echoing this theme, the secretary general of the MIR claimed that it was "the ruling classes that need a truce to develop their tactic of obstructionism. Nothing would be more dangerous or suicidal today than to give up the positions that have been achieved and initiate a truce."[41]

Pressures on the Christian Democrats from the Right were also clear. In a cable sent from Rome, Senator Fuentealba warned against these pressures:

There are sectors bent on producing the fatal outcome, involving the fall of the government in the shortest possible time. They are criminals. I have faith that my party will be able to abide by the principles and ideals that inspire it, ignoring those who today approach as friends, when in the past they sought the party's destruction.... [42]

From the very outset, attempts to reach a *modus vivendi* ran into difficulties.[43] When Allende asked the Christian Democrats to support a declaration of state of siege in the aftermath of the coup, the Christian Democratic Council met to consider the request. Some members argued that the party should give Allende an affirmative response and then qualify it by asking for certain guarantees against the abuse of power. This conciliatory stand received only four votes to the fourteen received by the harsher demand for a rejection of the government request until certain guarantees could be offered. Like a sovereign state receiving a delegation from another sovereign state, the council informed three of Allende's ministers of the decision. They did not return as scheduled to bring the government's reply. The published declaration of the Christian Democrats concluded by noticing that "once again, Christian Democracy thinks it necessary to stress before the people of Chile that the responsibility for bringing to an end the climate of disorder, insecurity and chaos to which the country has come and the extremely grave crisis in which it finds itself is primarily the responsibility of the President of the Republic."[44]

The president moved swiftly, however, to institute a new cabinet, relieving the ministers who had been impeached—a painful move for the Communist party. He worked hard at attempting to construct a cabinet of prestigious individuals, such as Felipe Herrera, the former president of the Inter-American Development Bank. He also sought out opposition figures such as Fernando Castillo.

The Christian Democrats, however, expressing the fear that Allende was trying to divide the party, refused to grant permission for their members to join the cabinet. Having failed to put together a bipartisan "blue ribbon" ministry, Allende proceeded to form one of a decidedly moderate character. As minister of the interior he named Carlos Briones, an independent Socialist considered to be a "man of law" in many circles. As minister of foreign relations, he kept Clodomiro Almeyda, one of the few Allende ministers to escape impeachment consistently. Senator Volodia Teitelboim, the leading ideologue of the Communist party, called the cabinet a "unity cabinet" designed to bring together all Chileans who wished to avoid the catastrophe of civil war, adding that the cabinet was an opening to dialogue.[45] At considerable risk to the unity of his own coalition, which was already experiencing significant erosion from the far Left, Allende continued to pursue the strategy of establishing a "minimum consensus" with the largest opposition party.

The leadership of the Christian Democrats did not respond readily to the president's overtures. It felt that Allende was being less than honest—that he was not really prepared to break with his extreme Left—and was merely buying time to implement his full program. At the same time, the leadership was under considerable pressure from a rightist faction intent on undermining Allende as much as possible. These elements were prepared to foster and join the escalating chorus of demands for the president's resignation. Party-affiliated gremios, unions, and local organizations added their numbers and voices to the crippling strikes which were rapidly reappearing. Many party members were in contact with military officers, giving tacit approval to plans for direct military action.

In late July, however, the cardinal, Raúl Silva Enriquez, employing all of the prestige of his office, urged a renewal of conversations between the antagonistic factions. Allende, in an emotional speech before the CUT, responded with a renewed appeal for talks. Defying many of the members of his party, who booed him at a mass meeting at party headquarters, Senator Patricio Aylwin, the Christian Democratic president, agreed to the conversations. The strong pressure on him was further evidenced by attacks on "dialogue" printed in the party paper, La Prensa.

Attempts were also being made behind the scenes to ensure the success of the talks. Gabriel Valdés, the highly regarded foreign minister in the Frei government, returned temporarily to Chile during July from his post at the United Nations.[46] After meeting with President Allende and top leaders of the Christian Democratic party, he was invited to a dinner at the home of Aniceto Rodriquez, a prominent leader of the moderate wing of the Socialist party. There he met with several cabinet ministers and prominent leaders of the Popular Unity coalition, who were anxious to hear from Valdés his views on a possible resolution of the crisis. They expressed real interest in establishing links at levels other than the highly public and formal dialogue of the president and the leader of the Christian Democrats. They also seemed willing to entertain the idea that a settlement might mean the incorporation of Christian Democrats in the cabinet, even at the risk of losing the support of a segment of the Socialist party. In turn, the Christian Democrats would have to respect much of the basic outline of the government program, even if in modified form. There seemed to be agreement that the crisis had reached a point where only drastic measures should be taken against all odds. And yet that very conversation was interrupted by a phone call summoning the minister of the interior. He was given the shocking news that Allende's own naval attaché had been assassinated. The fury of charges and counter-charges which followed in the press and the quickening pace of events drowned out further progress behind the scenes. The formal conversations were begun the following Monday, with little groundwork having been done and with enormous obstacles to success. The entire nation watched and waited.

The Christian Democratic leaders went into the talks with the conviction that Allende would have to abandon much of his program and cut his ties with the far Left if an agreement were to be worked out.[47] Allende, in turn, was reluctant to take that final step. After the CUT speech he told Gabriel Valdés that he had experienced the saddest day of his life, and that he had indeed broken with his own party. But shortly afterward he postponed the start of the talks, much to the chagrin of his own minister of the interior, in a last-ditch effort to get Socialist party compliance. The Christian Democrats immediately interpreted this change of heart as evidence of the president's inability to abandon the more extreme elements of his coalition. They did not understand that Allende simply was reluctant to take a step that would have signaled the end of the Popular Unity in the absence of clear assurance that the Christian Democrats would provide him with genuine backing. The president believed that Frei had been meeting with army officers and was in tacit agreement with those supporting a coup. Why should he isolate himself further by severing ties with his own people if important Christian Democrats wanted him out of office anyway? In this confusing atmosphere neither side knew what the other side really wanted; neither side was fully prepared to believe that, even if the other side were sincere, it would be able to keep its word. The political arena had been drastically reduced to a few men attempting to come up with a magic settlement, but these men no longer had full control of the social forces around them. Only a dramatic announcement from the talks might have averted the final denouement; it was not forthcoming.

Senator Aylwin and his colleagues entered the conversations fearing that Allende, with his great reputation for political maneuvering, might outsmart them. They felt an enormous pressure, not only from their constituents but from their adversary, not to give in too much—not to concede essential points. When Allende, in their first meeting, pulled out some fat folders and noted that agreement could be reached on many substantive issues, Aylwin felt that Allende was still stalling. He insisted on pinning the president down with several demands, including a demand that the president bring the military in at all levels of government. The opposition, he noted, needed guarantees of good faith. The president could not accept that; it would have meant a virtual abdication of his role as governor. Allende stressed the many bases for possible agreement, including his willingness to resolve the constitutional question in Congress by accepting most of the opposition's version of the amendment, on the condition that the same procedure not be used again so that Chile would not become a parliamentary regime. He argued further that it was the responsibility of the politicians to structure an understanding, to resolve the political impasse. Then, the military could be brought in as an arbiter.

The non-negotiable demand made by the Christian Democrats for the incorporation of the military into the government was criticized as too extreme by many prominent members of the party, who still felt that Chile's problem was not dictatorship but anarchy. Neither Allende nor the Christian Democratic leadership seemed fully to appreciate the enormous political constraints the other was under. In their dogged opposition the Christian Democrats were more fearful of what Allende might do than what the consequences might be to the entire system on which their party, more than others, depended. Many seemed convinced that the "constitutionalist" Chilean military might simply force the president to leave and turn things back to them again. They seemed to have forgotten the fate of other democrats and centrist groups, in other times and places, who had abdicated at the critical moment.

On 9 August 1973, with the breakdown of formal talks and a new and massive truckers' strike underway, Allende, much to the chagrin of the Left, moved to bring the military into his cabinet. He knew that he no longer had much choice. While trying to save face by taking this action after the talks had terminated, he had in fact given in to most of the opposition's demands. The Christian Democratic leadership was, however, not satisfied. After initially supporting the move, they rebuked the president for not going far enough and replacing officials at all levels of the government. Critics within the party argued that the Christian Democrats were being unreasonable in making further demands before the new cabinet was given a real chance and in the process undermining the position of the military officers who had agreed to join the cabinet under great duress. The politicians had gone beyond the point of no return. They had been unable to come up with a political solution to Chile's political problems, and now it was too late. As the politicians continued to trade charges and counter-charges, the armed forces had in fact assumed authority over the country. It was only a matter of time before the *golpista* factions would be able to consolidate their plans to replace the elected government by force.

The Military on Its Own: The Fear of a Parallel Army and of Insurrection in the Ranks

The 29 June 1973 coup attempt was not the beginning of direct involvement of military officers in politics. From the early coup attempts before Allende took office until the fall of the Popular Unity government elements within the military plotted to overthrow the regime. But it was not until the 29 June incident, when a small tank regiment moved on the presidential palace, that an actual attempt took place. The *tanquetazo* was not a response to a general plan to take over the government. Rather, it was a move by a disgruntled officer, about to be relieved of his command, in the mistaken belief that discontent in the rest of the armed forces would lead to a rapidly escalating military takeover.[48] General Prats was able to move swiftly and easily, with little loss of life, to put down the insurrection, thus demonstrating that the "constitutionalist" sector in the military, particularly in the army, still had the upper hand. Yet the mere fact that a regiment of the highly professional Chilean army would move without direct orders from superiors provided tangible evidence of the mounting discontent among middle-ranking officers. The statements in the government press to the effect that the June coup had been a clear triumph for Allende ignored the depth of discontent in military ranks. It was significant that the dead rebels, as well as the dead loyalists, were buried with full military honors by an institution bent on ignoring the chants of Popular Unity adherents who cried, "Firing squad, firing squad."[49]

The abortive attempt had a profound impact on the armed services. In the political vacuum left by a weakened government struggling to achieve a compromise with the opposition, the military would increasingly strike out on its own in an attempt to control what was perceived to be the growing military threat of the Left. In the process a series of events would lead to the eventual loss of authority of the leading "constitutionalists" and their replacement by officers willing to move against the government.

It must be stressed that while there was conspiratorial planning at various levels, the coup was not a highly coordinated affair arranged weeks in advance. Rather, it was the result of a gradual and haphazard process.[50] This was the case because the Chilean military was a highly professional organization with a tremendous respect for discipline and the hierarchy of rank. It was not possible for middle-level officers of various services to stage a "colonel's coup" by mobilizing a few regiments. The abortive 29 June coup had vividly demonstrated that. For the coup to take place it would be necessary not only to structure a substantial consensus among high-ranking officers but also to see to it that the commanding officer of each service was in agreement with the final action. And, until the very end, in every service, the commanding officers were committed constitutionalists. In particular, General Prats and Admiral Montero strongly, and, for a time, successfully, resisted the pressures of their colleagues. General Ruiz Danyau, while more supportive of the neutrality of the military than most of his other air force colleagues, would bend more readily to pressure. Removal of a commanding officer was a tedious and frustrating process, because in the final analysis it could result only from action by the president of the republic or from a voluntary resignation approved by the president of the republic. It is instructive that it was not until the three generals in question were removed from their posts with presidential consent, albeit grudging, that the golpistas were able to push to a final military solution.

The importance of hiearchy and the respect for rank is illustrated by the formation after the 29 June incident of a committee of fifteen of the highest-ranking officers from the three services to discuss common problems and prepare for the possibility that Allende might invite the military into the cabinet. The three commanders in chief presided, and other officers sat around the table in order of seniority. In the 30 June meeting, General Pinochet, second in seniority to Prats, noted that it would be inappropriate to refer to political matters and that the officers should remain neutral and discuss economic problems. Though the officers drafted a twenty-nine-point memorandum critical of the national situation that was to be submitted to the president for discussion, it was clear that any talk of military insurrection was simply out of the question.[51]

It must also be underscored that the success of the golpistas in undermining the constitutionalists was not merely a response to an intramilitary debate isolated from the evolving situation in the country. In fact two sets of developments had a profound effect on the internal correlation of forces in the military. The first was the already noted failure of the politicians to reach a consensus which would force Allende to structure a new military cabinet in an atmosphere in which direct calls for military takeover were the order of the day. But even more significant was the escalation of *direct* confrontation between the military and elements of the Left. This took the form of growing fear within the armed forces that for the first time the institution itself was threatened. Officers were worried that the Left planned to set up a parallel military force among workers and, even more ominously, instigate widespread insubordination among the troops.[52]

Though elements within the armed forces undoubtedly feared statements coming from the revolutionary Left about armed workers, it was not until after the attempted coup that military men began to show active concern over the development of a parallel army. The government had given wide publicity to the attempt at mobilization of the cordones industriales around Santiago as soon as the tanks started rolling.[53] After 29 June, leftist sectors of the Popular Unity coalition, while criticizing efforts of the government to compromise with the opposition, called for mass mobilization and arming of the workers. In a speech the secretary general of the socialist party noted:

The workers of the whole country have organized in cordones industriales, communal commandos, peasant councils, committees of vigilance and other organizations, which constitute the seeds of an incipient but powerful popular force, and are an unbreachable barrier before any insurrectionary attempts of the bourgeoisie. Workers, peasants, neighborhood dwellers, young people, all are amassing their own power to repel the mutinous power of the bourgeois. And they have the obligation to do just that as a class and as a revolutionary movement.[54]

At around the same time Miguel Enriquez, head of the MIR, observed that

The working class is today a structured army, bent on fighting for its interests and resisting the onslaught of the reactionaries. The working class and the people . . . have given notice to their political leadership that the struggle has left the corridors of parliament and that they will not permit setbacks or concessions.[55]

The leader of the Communist party also argued that "If the reactionary sedition becomes worse, passing into the area of armed struggle, no one should doubt that the people will rise as one man to crush it with speed."[56] At the same time, a widely distributed pamphlet urged the workers to

Develop at an accelerated pace the acomplishment of military tasks in the party and among the masses . . . . Form organizations necessary to assure the self defense of the masses in industries, services, neighborhoods, communes, and cordones, developing "armed popular power" and developing the bases for the construction of the future Army of the People.[57]

Ironically, the militant rhetoric of leaders on the Left was in part due to the fact that the 29 June movement had shown the response of the working class to be less than overwhelming. Only a handful of cordones had taken over factories. Most of the Left had stood by and watched General Prats put down the revolt.[58] In view of the poor showing of the Left, revolutionary elements wanted to accelerate the arming of the workers to be better prepared for another attempted coup. Yet their attempt to ensure a better "defense" of the working class led to a concerted determination on the part of the armed forces to prevent that very development.[59] The weakness of the cordones had also been observed by many officers who, nevertheless, had been rudely awakened to the potential of working-class resistance. They quickly turned to a law, which had been on the books for some time, giving the armed forces authority over control of arms in order to assure themselves that a parallel army would not be created.

The first significant military raid came as early as 8 July in the Metropolitan Cemetery, when the air force led a large raid in search of weapons. The government press immediately attacked the raid and ridiculed the air force for not finding any weapons. In a televised interview the commander of the air force showed his annoyance, particularly against a leftist newspaper partly owned by the minister of defense. At the same time, in a clear demonstration of the rift between the military and the government, he vehemently attacked the undersecretary of the interior's contention that no weapons were found in the raid.

Actions by the air force were followed by similar efforts by the navy in the port city of Valparaíso. In two weeks naval forces carried out over twenty raids in search of weapons. Despite the fact that rightist groups were also armed, the raids were aimed at factories in the social sector and particularly at those in the hands of Socialist party militants. Again the commander in chief of the navy clashed with the undersecretary of the interior. When military officers raided a worker's federation headquarter in Osorno, the secretary general of the CUT sharply criticized the arms control law, calling it the "damned law," a term coined by the MIR.

By August the government no longer controlled the actions of the armed forces. Allende could only observe helplessly as the military broke into government factories and party headquarters. In Concepción the navy conducted a number of raids against suspected leftist arsenals. While dangerous materials were occasionally discovered, more often they were found in agencies such as the Highway Department and the Development Corporation, both of which stored explosives for routine work. Probably the worst incident of military search-and-destroy operations took place in the southern city of Punta Arenas. The army broke into a factory and apparently destroyed machinery and killed a worker in its search for weapons. The attack on the army from the Left became so vehement that Allende personally had to instruct elements of his coalition to keep the criticism down.

The fear of a parallel army also contributed to a refinement of the many contingency plans which the armed forces had long since developed to enable them to act in concert to control domestic insurgency. The air force, fearing possible damage to some of its aircraft from the Los Cerrillos Cordones, which was located near the military airport, obtained the support of marines to guard the planes and transferred many planes to other cities without presidential approval. It would not be difficult to turn the machinery set up to root out illegal arms to the broader goal of destroying the government.[60]

With the 29 June attempted coup, parties of the extreme Left called not only for formation of armed groups which would be prepared to fight the next coup but for the open resistance of enlisted men to those officers who did not fully support the government. All around Santiago, posters went up urging soldiers not to take orders in the event of military action. The head of the Socialist party argued publicly that

Soldiers, marines, air force men, and police can't serve as tools at any time and under any circumstance for the assassination of workers. And if the case should come up again, officers, noncommissioned officers, and rank-and-file soldiers have the obligation not to obey. What is even clearer: not only do they have a duty to disobey orders which would mean shooting at the people . . . they must actively oppose any such action. We are sure that this patriotic stand, national and revolutionary, will prevail over the desperate maneuvers of the bourgeoisie.[61]

Almost immediately after the attempted coup, officers began to purge the ranks of elements viewed as sympathetic to the government. This was particularly true in the navy. On 7 August the navy denounced a plot, coordinated by the MIR and factions of the Socialist party, to take over several ships. The navy argued that the Left was deliberately fostering insurrection in the ranks. The Left, in turn, argued that this was necessary in order to counter the open plotting among naval officers. The navy accompanied its announcement of internal difficulties with renewed raids all over the Concepción area in search of arms, a call for denial of congressional immunity to top Popular Unity leaders, and the issuance of an order of detention against the secretary general of the MIR. These events placed the government in an untenable situation. It simply could not arrest those who argued that they were doing their best to protect the government from a coup. On the other hand, the activities of leftist leaders among rank-and-file army personnel further reinforced the resolve of those intent on staging a coup and seriously undermined the position of those officers, particularly Admiral Montero, who continued to argue that the armed forces should remain neutral.[62] For a majority of officers, it was no longer a matter of objecting to erroneous government policies but a matter of defending themselves and their institutions from the possibility of destruction.

The Military Cabinet and the Triumph of the Hard Liners

With the failure of the talks with the Christian Democrats, and the failure of his thesis that the politicians should resolve the fundamental difficulties before turning elsewhere, Allende turned to the armed forces to create a cabinet of "national security." In so doing he fully accepted the points prepared by the military committee of fifteen as condition for their entry into the cabinet. In a 6 August meeting, both General Prats and Admiral Montero indicated willingness to join the cabinet. They felt strongly about the need to resolve the political crisis within the framework of the Chilean constitution. For General Ruiz the situation was more difficult; the pressure from his fellow generals not to enter the government was intense. General Prats became defense minister, Admiral Montero went to the Ministry of Finance and General Ruiz to the Ministry of Public Works. The other ministries were filled by moderate leaders of the UP with Orlando Letelier in the Ministry of the Interior.

In inaugurating his new cabinet, the president openly criticized the attempt by elements on the revolutionary Left to infiltrate the armed forces. He also had to intervene personally to break up a strike in the Ministry of Public Works and Transport so that General Ruiz could take over as minister, charged among other things with the difficult task of settling the ongoing and paralyzing truckers' strike. For all intents and purposes Allende had broken with his Socialist colleagues.[63]

But from the very outset the military cabinet was in deep trouble. The chorus of demands for the president's resignation had now become thunderous. The Christian Democrats, instead of interpreting the president's move as fulfilling their earlier demands, criticized it vehemently for not going far enough. The truckers and other striking organizations were clearly no longer interested in negotiating. With ample financial support from external sources, they were content to wait and force a presidential resignation or a military coup.[64] Though the president was willing to dismiss the undersecretary of the ministry, whom opposition groups blamed for the lack of a settlement in the truckers' strike, it no longer made much difference. The Christian Democrats strongly supported the strikers. The military was once again caught in the middle. A deafening outcry from the opposition called on them to be firm and not to give into the government. The National party openly called for a coup. The revolutionary Left, possessed of ample evidence of plotting at middle levels of the military, sought desperately to consolidate a military posture, thereby only aggravating military insecurity. Sabotage from right-wing groups escalated. On 13 August three high-tension pylons outside of Santiago were dynamited, interrupting a presidential speech and cutting off power in the center of the country for an hour. Shortly thereafter General Ruiz resigned and was succeeded as commander in chief by General Gustavo Leigh and as minister of public works and transport by General Humberto Magliochetti. The air force generals made it clear once again that there was little support for the government from their quarter. Doctors, lawyers, teachers, and engineers joined the antigovernment strikes.

The most serious blow yet to the government came on 22 August when General Prats finally resigned. His resignation came after a curious incident in which the wives of many fellow officers demonstrated outside his home. Soon after that a majority of the generals asked him to resign to ensure "unity" in the armed forces. Prominent among the anti-Prats generals were Generals Oscar Bonilla and Sergio Arellano, who were known to have close ties with sectors of the Christian Democratic party. This reinforced the view among Popular Unity leaders that some Christian Democrats, including former president Frei, tacitly supported a military solution.[65]

The same day the Chamber of Deputies, with support from the Christian Democrats, adopted a "sense of the House" resolution which held that the government of President Allende was unconstitutional, all but inviting a military coup.[66] More than ever the opposition seemed to be openly inciting action. To the relief of the president, General Augusto Pinochet, who was closely identified with Prats, gave strong assurances to the government that the army would continue to remain neutral and pledged support to ensure loyalty at all levels. On 28 August Allende named a new and final cabinet with Carlos Briones as the minister of the interior.

What finally sealed the fate of the Popular Unity government, however, was the successful attempt of the navy to obtain the resignation of Admiral

Montero.[67] For some time many of his fellow admirals had been urging him to resign. On 29 August Admiral Jose Toribio Merino, second in command, and Admiral Sergio Huidobro, commanding officer of the naval infantry, went to see Montero to convey the opinion of the Naval Council that he should step down. Montero immediately called the president, who insisted that all three come over to see him. A bitter exchange took place in which the president told Merino that he knew that he was "at war" with the navy. On the first of September all of the admirals were summoned to the office of the minister of defense, Orlando Letelier, to explain one by one why they felt Montero must resign. Finally, after often tearful sessions with his colleagues, Montero asked to be relieved of his post. Allende also relented and agreed to let the admiral give way to a successor on 7 September. (The president would later try fruitlessly for six hours to convince Admiral Merino in person to pledge support for the government.)

The whole political system had been reduced to the president and a few trusted colleagues, moving from crisis to crisis, minute by minute, twenty-four hours a day, attempting to cajole and convince others to postpone what now seemed inevitable. Many of the same officers who later would authorize the merciless persecution of Allende's friends and followers spent hours in personal conversations with the president himself. Allende had also been in touch with the president of the Christian Democrats in a futile attempt to head off the damaging vote in the Chamber of Deputies. At the same time, he was carrying on extensive negotiations with elements of his own coalition in an attempt to forge another political solution. The device decided on was a plebiscite, to be held during the second week of September, calling for the election of a constitutional assembly to resolve the crisis. The Communist party was intent on the move, and secretary general Luis Corvalán supported it vigorously.[68] To Corvalán's irritation, Allende insisted on trying to bring the balking Socialists around to his position, though he was determined to proceed without their support if necessary. Through the good offices of the cardinal, the Christian Democrats were approached directly to obtain their reaction to the plebiscite proposal. General Pinochet and other army generals Allende deemed loyal were informed of his plan on 7 September. Over the weekend the minister of the interior and others worked frantically to come up with the wording for the president's speech, announcing the plebiscite, and they still had legal problems to resolve the night of 10 September.

But the coup was already in progress. Over the same weekend top naval officers met in Valparaíso to coordinate their activities, confident that elements within the army were in favor and that General Pinochet was now willing to go along. To make absolutely certain that the other services were in agreement, two high-ranking naval officers set out for Santiago and, incredibly, had to return to Valparaíso because they had forgotten to take money for the highway toll. After some delay they were able to fulfill their mission. Generals Leigh and Pinochet signed a document prepared by Admiral Merino setting the date of the coup for 11 September 1973.[69]

The shift in the army appeared to be a last-minute shift on the part of General Pinochet. A large number of lower-ranking army officers had that same week personally called Orlando Letelier, the minister of defense, to invite their former colleague from military academy days to a banquet for more than ninety officers the following week. They spoke cordially with the new minister of defense, hardly reflecting the mood of a military organization already geared up to destroy the government and arrest its top leaders, including the minister of defense. With the shift of General Pinochet, however, the professional institution quickly fell into line, sealing the fate of the Popular Unity government.[70]

On Tuesday of the following week, the military moved quickly to depose the elected government. The presidential palace and the president's private residence became the central targets of bombs and army troops. Allende died in his presidential office, the first of many victims of a military coup aimed not at "restoring" institutions and democratic procedures but at dismantling them with brutality and vengeance. The real transformation of Chilean politics began not on 4 September 1970 but on 11 September 1973.

Conclusion

The 1970 presidential election brought into office, for the first time in Chilean history, a minority coalition dominated by Marxist parties dedicated to a fundamental transformation of that country's economic, social, and political structures. From the outset, the experiment of President Salvador Allende encountered a multiplicity of constraints inherent in Chile's highly polarized political system. The government sought to change the economy and redistribute income on short notice, without abandoning the traditional politics of *reivindicaciones*. Government parties struggled over different ideological programs while continuing to engage in competitive electoral politics. In a highly dialectical process, elements wedded to both the social and political status quo reacted with vigor at any encroachment on their privileges. The polarized system became even more polarized as zero-sum elections and the pressure of electoral competition contributed to an erosion of the tenuous Center. Structural constraints were accompanied by symbolic contraints. An escalation of rhetoric on both sides made it difficult for leaders committed to the ongoing system to perceive and understand what was going on. It is clear that this crisis was fundamentally a political crisis, and the political crisis in Chile preceded the socioeconomic crisis. In time mobilization would get out of hand, but it was the counter-mobilization of those who felt threatened in a system which lost authority which finally contributed to the breakdown of Chilean democracy.

Given the characteristics of the Chilean system which structured human action, the Chilean breakdown followed, at an ever-faster pace, the path described by Juan Linz in his analysis of earlier European breakdowns. The challenge from elements openly disloyal to the traditional democratic regime turned out to be less important than the abdication of erstwhile supporters caught in the crossfire from both extremes. Leaders chose to protect narrow personal stakes, defined by the requirements of electoral advantage, refusing to see the importance of preserving the regime itself.

There is little doubt that the pressures on the democrats in the Center to maintain a viable consensus were enormous. Both sides often complained about these pressures and difficulties, and yet each side failed to see the gravity of the pressures on those of the opposite side. Their actions only worsened the situation and, by implication, the prospects for a successful regime-saving compromise.

Allende was often too willing to bow to the pressures from the Left and continuously gave ambivalent cues. He thus undermined, in the early stage of his government, the position of those elements of the opposition who were genuinely interested in reaching an agreement that would not involve a threat to the Popular Unity coalition's basic program. The corruption and disorder in the political process and the "unsolvable problem" of the economy only made things more difficult. The Christian Democrats, in turn, were intimidated by the political threat both from the Right and from many of their own followers, and were obsessed with the notion of presenting a hard-line posture to the very end. They should have realized more fully the necessity of coming to an agreement when the government coalition was willing, in the crucial negotiations of June and July 1972. But, even more seriously, they should have realized that the political game shifted dramatically in the last stage of the Popular Unity government with the outcome of the 1973 elections and the attempted coup of 29 June of that year. In combating the dubious prospect of "Marxist totalitarianism," to the bitter end, they failed to realize how much of a stake they had in the democratic political order they thought they were defending. By not moving forcefully to structure a political solution, they seriously undermined the position of the president and his advisers, who were clearly ready to reach a mutual accommodation. In the chaotic atmosphere of mid-1973 this failure only undermined further the authority of the government and the increasingly powerless leadership of the political elites themselves. The resulting mobilization and countermobilization, used to demonstrate power capabilities, became an indicator of loss of real power. The resort to so-called neutral powers only led to a fatal reliance on the armed forces to "solve" the crisis. And contrary to the expectations of some naive "democrats," including many prominent Christian Democrats, Chile's armed forces did not merely see to it that an "unconstitutional" president was removed from office: they dispensed with the constitution altogether.

But the moderates of the Center were not the only ones who misinterpreted Chilean political reality. The scenario of the revolutionary Left was also an illusory one. The leftists blamed the government for not accelerating the political process in order to force a confrontation that would have led to working-class victory and a genuine Socialist revolution. Ironically, while the Christian Democrats and the Nationals were attacking the government for setting the stage for a dictatorship of the Left, the revolutionary Left was just as vehemently attacking the government for failing to move in that direction. The assumptions of the revolutionary Left were two-fold. In the first place, they were convinced that the working class, given the proper direction, was ready to join in a militant challenge which might involve armed class struggle. And secondly, they assumed that during the first period of the Popular Unity government, the "reactionary forces" were divided and the military was neutral, so that a massive and rapid effort to mobilize the working class would find little resistance. From an analysis of the Chilean case it is clear, however, that it would not have been possible to overcome, in two short years, the basically economic aspirations of the working class and to infuse them with revolutionary class consciousness. Workers in Chile expected to better their lot in life under the new government; they would not have given their lives for a revolution which many of them thought had already come.

But it is quite evident from a study of the Chilean case that the second assumption was also untenable. The opposition was divided in the early years of the Allende administration because progressive sectors of the opposition were willing to support the government; indeed, they enabled the government to come to power in the first place. It is absurd to think that they would have remained supportive or neutral had the government embarked on an unequivocal strategy of accelerating class conflict. The countermobilization which occurred in the end would simply have occurred sooner. Even more significantly, there was no support in the armed forces for a revolutionary strategy which would have tolerated the mobilization of armed workers. The government was able to stave off military interference for as long as it did precisely because it stuck to basic constitutional procedures. Had Allende and his colleagues moved dramatically in 1971 to "consolidate power," the golpista faction in the armed forces would have materialized much sooner. Even if the working class had been more revolutionary than it was, it would have been impossible in 1971 (as it was in 1973) to mount a military force capable of challenging the highly professional Chilean military.

The fact is that the revolutionary Left, by attempting to radicalize the political process, contributed in substantial measure to undermining the very success of the government's so-called *Via Chilena* strategy. By its actions, the revolutionary Left, which had always ridiculed the possibility of a Socialist transformation through peaceful means, was engaged in a self-fulfilling prophecy.

It is clear that any agreement to structure a compromise to preserve the Chilean system would have entailed acceptance by the Popular Unity coalition of progressive changes, many of which would have fallen short of original goals. The Christian Democrats would, in turn, have had to accept a more fundamental transformation of the ongoing system than many would have wanted. It is also likely that an agreement would have involved a curtailment of the activities of some groups of the revolutionary Left.

The key is not that such a development would have precluded a revolutionary transformation. A fundamental and early Socialist revolution in Chile was simply out of the question anyway. The tragic dilemma of Chile today is that it must now live with a third alternative which is far worse for most of the political actors on the Chilean stage and for the bulk of the population: a reactionary military government. Christian Democrats now realize that the threat of the Allende government was nothing compared to the systematic denial of basic political freedoms and human rights under the rule of General Pinochet. Elections have been banned, electoral registers burned, and scores of party leaders arrested, harassed, or exiled. The party has lost its organs of information and is unable to express its views, let alone provide an alternative for leadership. The Left, of course, has suffered much more. Many of its leaders have been tortured and killed. Militants and their followers have been systematically harassed, deprived of their jobs and their livelihoods. Union leaders have been arrested and relieved of their positions. The revolutionary Left has been decimated and some of its most prominent leaders killed in real and alleged confrontations. Certainly their lot is far worse today than it was under political democracy. The courts, who argued so eloquently for human rights when there was no real threat, have shamefully acquiesced in a violation of human rights without precedent in Chile's history as an independent nation.

The Chilean experience has shown how easy it is for a professional and "neutral" military to become a repressive military regime. As soon as the military defined fellow countrymen as enemies against whom all-out war had to be waged, every conceivable repressive measure became justifiable. It is not surprising that the military has acted like an occupation force and treated the whole nation as if it were a giant regiment. It is also natural for an institution that thrives on hierarchy, order, and discipline to consider political democracy anathema to a war effort. In fact, the military leaders have explicitly blamed democracy for allowing "foreign" forces to corrupt a segment of the Chilean people. In order to "heal" the nation they have sought to extirpate all of those policies which in some way can be identified with a weak democracy and Marxist forces. Thus they have gone beyond banning political rights and persecuting people, and have dismantled reforms, not only of the Allende administration, but reforms won democratically over the years by progressive forces. Rights to strike, to job security, to education, and to good health have been severely restricted by a regime so obsessed with national security that the only ones to benefit from its policies are those sectors of the population identified with large Chilean and foreign business enterprises. The absence of political brokers and mechanisms of accountability means that little redress can be obtained, not only for the more flagrant political wrongs but for the everyday injustices that countless Chileans suffer at the hands of faceless and distant public and private bureaucracies. Even the gremios, who so vociferously called for the overthrow of Allende, now find their channels of access blocked and their traditional methods of protest curtailed.

It is still too early to tell what will happen in Chile. In their effort to obtain a better and more just society or to maintain the values they held dear, Chileans contributed to the destruction of a unique system of government. The coup of 1973 was followed by such widespread killing and repression that it will probably be impossible to restructure in quite the same way institutions and procedures which had evolved over generations. The problem is not only that it will be difficult for the military junta to step down because of the inevitable demands for retaliation. The main difficulty may very well be one of structuring the centrist consensus which proved to be so elusive in the last years of Chilean political democracy. So far, representatives of the various Chilean factions seem more intent on vindicating their actions and previous positions than on seeking to build bridges to the future.[71]

Notes

INTRODUCTION

1. Most scholars point to the leadership of Diego Portales, a cabinet minister in the late 1830s, as the most important influence on the development of stable republican institutions in Chile. The literature on the Portales period is very extensive. The reader is referred to the following works as particularly useful ones: Ramón Sotomayor Valdés, *Historia de Chile bajo gobierno del General D. Joaquín Prieto*, 3d ed. (Santiago: Fondo Histórico Presidente Joaquín Prieto, 1962); Francisco Antonio Encina, *Portales*, 2 vols. (Santiago: Editorial Nascimiento, 1964); Diego Barros Arana, *Un decenio de la historia de Chile*, 2 vols. (Santiago: Imprenta Universitaria, 1906); Aurelio Díaz Meza, *El advenimiento de Portales* (Santiago: Ediciones Ercilla, 1932). A classic study of the economy and economic policies during the period is Daniel Martner, *Historia de Chile: Historia económica*, vol. 1 (Santiago: Balcells and Co., 1929). Among the best general works for understanding the period, and which, for the most part, praise Portales, are Alberto Edwards Vives, *La fronda aristocrática* (Santiago: Editorial Ercilla, 1936); and Luis Galdames, *History of Chile* (Chapel Hill: University of North Carolina Press, 1941). Critical assessments of Portales come both from liberal and Marxist historians who condemn the nineteenth-century Chilean state as serving in an autocratic fashion the interests of the landed aristocracy. Among liberal historians, see Ricardo Donoso, *Desarrollo político y social de Chile desde la constitución de 1833* (Santiago: Imprenta Universitaria, 1942); and idem, *Las ideas políticas en Chile*, 2d ed. (Santiago: Editorial Universitaria, S.A., 1967). Among Marxists, see Julio Cesar Jobet, *Ensayo Crítico del desarrollo económico y social de Chile* (Santiago: Editorial Universitaria, 1955). Both critics and admirers of Portales agree that he was responsible for establishing the institutional structure of nineteenth-century Chile. Some authors have recently questioned the view that Portales was singlehandedly responsible for the course of Chilean democracy. For example, see Jay Kinsbruner, *Diego Portales: Interpretative Essays on the Man and Times* (The Hague: Martinus Nijhoff, 1967). Arturo Valenzuela believes that a succession of events, including the war against the Perú-Bolivia confederation and the character of the Bulnes presidency, must be taken into account in analyzing the Chilean "deviant case." See Arturo Valenzuela, *Political Brokers in Chile: Local Government in a Centralized Polity* (Durham, N.C.: Duke University Press, 1977).

2. For a discussion of this thesis see Claudio Véliz, "La Mesa de tres patas," *Desarrollo Económico* 3, nos. 1–2 (April-September 1963): 173–230. This theme is also discussed in Armand Mattelart, Carmen Castillo, and Leonardo Castillo, *La ideología de la dominacíon en una sociedad dependiente* (Buenos Aires: Ediciones Signos, 1970); Norbert Lechner, *La democracia en Chile* (Buenos Aires: Ediciones Signos, 1970); and Julio Samuel Valenzuela, "The Determinants of Suffrage Expansion in Chile: The 1874 Law" (unpublished paper, Columbia University, 1972).

3. An excellent article on the historiography of the civil war of 1891 is Harold Blakemore, "The Chilean Revolution of 1891 and Its Historiography," *Hispanic American Historical Review* 45, no. 3 (August 1965): 393–421. Standard interpretations of the war stress either the ideology and personality of Balmaceda and congressional actors or the institutional conflict between the presidency and Congress. Marxist scholars such as Hernán Ramírez Necochea have put forth a revisionary interpretation. Ramírez argues that Balmaceda was a nationalist intent on placing the nitrate industry in Chilean hands. He was opposed by foreign (British) nitrate interests who, in effect, were able to buy off elements in the Chilean

111

Congress. See his *Balmaceda y la contrarrevolución de 1891*, 2d rev. ed. (Santiago: Editorial Universitaria, 1969). While both interpretations have considerable merit, this author believes that a third interpretation, stressing the important center-local struggle, deserves much more attention. See Valenzuela, *Political Brokers in Chile*, chap. 8.

4. General discussions of the evolution of Chilean political parties include Galdames, *A History of Chile*; Federico Gil, *The Political System of Chile* (Boston: Houghton Mifflin Co., 1966); Alberto Edwards and Eduardo Frei, *Historia de los partidos políticos chilenos* (Santiago: Editorial del Pacífico, 1949); Germán Urzúa Valenzuela, *Los partidos políticos chilenos* (Santiago: Editorial Jurídica de Chile, 1968); Sergio Guilisati Tagle, *Partidos políticos chilenos* (Santiago: Editorial Nascimiento, 1964).

5. For studies describing the repression of labor, see Hernán Ramírez Necochea, *Historia del movimiento obrero. Siglo XIX. Antecedentes* (Santiago: Talleres Gráficos Lautaro, 1956) and Julio José Jobet, *Ensayo crítico del desarrollo económico social de Chile* (Santiago: Editorial Universitaria, 1955).

6. However, in 1948, the middle-class parties shifted to an alliance with the Right and banned the Communist party, fearing the increased electoral strength of the Left. For references see n. 10, chap. 1.

7. See Juan Linz, *The Breakdown of Democratic Regimes: Crisis, Breakdown, and Reequilibration* (Baltimore, Md.: Johns Hopkins University Press, 1978).

CHAPTER 1

1. Federico Gil, *The Political System of Chile* (Boston: Houghton Mifflin Co., 1966), p. 244.

2. The survey was conducted in Santiago, Chile, in mid-1958 by Eduardo Hamuy. Raw data were obtained from the International Data Library and Reference Service, Survey Research Center, University of California, Berkeley. Chapter 1 of this study draws extensively on the author's "Political Constraints and the Prospects for Socialism in Chile," *Proceedings of the Academy of Political Science* 30, no. 4 (August 1972): 65–82.

3. On Chilean electoral law, see Mario Bernaschina, *Cartilla electoral* (Santiago: Editorial Jurídica, 1958). For the 1962 electoral law and its 1965 and 1968 modifications, see Antonio Vodanovic, ed., *Ley general de elecciones* (Santiago: Editorial Nascimiento, 1969). In 1970 a constitutional amendment was adopted giving illiterates the right to vote and lowering the voting age to eighteen. It took effect in time for the 1971 municipal election. For the legislative history of the amendment and its text, see Guillermo Piedrabuena Richards, *La reforma constitucional* (Santiago: Ediciones Encina, 1970).

4. All electoral information appearing in this chapter is derived from raw data obtained primarily in mimeograph form from the Dirección del Registro Electoral, Santiago, Chile.

5. See Arturo Valenzuela, "The Scope of the Chilean Party System," *Comparative Politics* 4, no. 2 (January 1972): 179–99. Data from Chile lead to a rejection of an influential body of literature in the social sciences which suggests that underdeveloped communities are less politically differentiated. For example, see S. N. Eisenstadt, "Social Change, Differentiation, and Evolution," *American Sociological Review* 29, no. 3 (June 1964): 375–87.

6. On the Chilean Right, see Ignacio Arteaga Undurraga, comp., *Partido Conservador XIV-Convención Nacional-1947* (Santiago: Imprenta Chile, 1947), which includes sketches of all conservative conventions from 1878 to 1947, lists of legislators and cabinet officers belonging to the party from 1831 to 1949, the party platform, and general notes on the 1947 convention. See also Marcial Sanfuentes Carrión, *El Partido Conservador* (Santiago: Editorial Universitaria, 1957), and José Miguel Prado Valdés, *Reseña histórica del Partido Liberal* (Santiago: Imprenta Andina, 1963). A very valuable reference to the numerous parties and party fragments spanning the ideological spectrum is Lía Cortés and Jordi Fuentes, *Diccionario político de Chile* (Santiago: Editorial Orbe, 1967).

7. Books on the Chilean Left are numerous. For a sampling, see Julio Cesar Jobet, *El Partido Socialista de Chile*, 2d ed., 2 vols. (Santiago: Ediciones Prensa Latinoamericana, 1971); Raúl Ampuero, *La izquierda en punto muerto*, 3d ed. (Santiago: Editorial Orbe 1969); Salomón Corbalán, *El Partido Socialista* (Santiago: Imprenta Atenea, 1957); Alejandro

Chelén Rojas, *Trayectoria del socialismo* (Buenos Aires: Editorial Austral, 1967); Hernán Ramírez Necochea, *Origen y formación del Partido Communista de Chile* (Santiago: Editorial Austral, 1965); Luis Corvalán Lepe, *Camino de victoria* (Santiago: Sociedad Impresora Horizonte, 1971); Ernst Halperin, *Nationalism and Communism in Chile* (Cambridge, Mass.: MIT Press, 1965).

8. For studies of the Chilean Radical party, see Luis Palma Zuñiga, *Historia del Partido Radical* (Santiago: Editorial Andrés Bello, 1967); Florencio Durán Bernales, *El Partido Radical* (Santiago: Editorial Nascimiento, 1958); Germán Urzúa Valenzuela, *El Partido Radical: Su evolución política* (Santiago: Academia de Ciencias Políticas y Administrativas, 1961). On the Christian Democrats, see Leonard Gross, *The Last Best Hope: Eduardo Frei and Chilean Christian Democracy* (New York: Random House, 1967); George Grayson, *El Partido Demócrata Cristiano Chileno* (Buenos Aires: Editorial Francisco de Aguirre, 1968); Eduardo Frei Montalva, *Pensamiento y acción* (Santiago: Editorial del Pacífico, 1958); Jaime Castillo Velasco, *Las fuentes de la Democracia Cristiana,* 2d ed. (Santiago: Editorial del Pacífico, 1968); Arturo Olavarría Bravo, *Chile bajo la Democracia Cristiana* (Santiago: Editorial Nascimiento, 1966); Suzanne Bodenheimer, "Stagnation in Liberty," in *North American Congress on Latin America; New Chile* (Berkeley: NACLA, 1972): 118–29; Arpad von Lazar and Luis Quiróz Varela, "Chilean Christian Democracy: Lessons in the Politics of Reform Management," *Inter-American Economic Affairs* 21, no. 4 (Spring 1968): 51–72.

9. "Public Opinion and the Movement of the Chilean Government to the Left, 1952–1972," in Arturo Valenzuela and J. Samuel Valenzuela, *Chile: Politics and Society* (New Brunswick, N.J.: Transaction, Inc., 1976), pp. 67–114.

10. President Gabriel Gonzalez Videla conveyed his concern about the Communist electoral success directly to party leader Volodia Teiltelboim when he told him, the day after the 1947 municipal election, that "I cannot permit the Communist party to achieve power through democratic channels." See the citation in Ampuero, *La izquierda en punto muerto*, p. 24. A discussion of the outlawing of the Communist party can be found in Chelén Rojas, *Trayectoria del socialismo*, pp. 114–19. A fascinating discussion of the controversial election of 1938 which brought the Popular Front into office is contained in Marta Infante Barros, *Testigos del treinta y ocho* (Santiago: Editorial Andrés Bello, 1972).

11. On the Radical years, see John R. Stevenson, *The Chilean Popular Front* (Philadelphia: The University of Pennsylvania Press, 1942); Alberto Baltra Cortés, *Pedro Aguirre Cerda* (Santiago: Editorial Orbe, 1962); Alberto Cabero, *Recuerdos de don Pedro Aguirre Cerda* (Santiago: Editorial Nascimiento, 1948). See also Arturo Olavarría Bravo, *Chile entre dos Alessandri*, 2 vols. (Santiago: Editorial Nascimiento, 1962).

12. A good account of the Ibañez period remains to be written. See general works such as Gil, *Political System of Chile*; Alberto Edwards and Eduardo Frei, *Historia de los partidos político chilenos*; (Santiago: Editorial del Pacífico, 1949); and Ricardo Donoso, *Desarrollo político y social de Chile* (Santiago: Imprenta Universitaria, 1943).

13. See Giovanni Sartori, "European Political Parties: The Case of Polarized Pluralism," in *Political Parties and Political Development,* ed. Joseph Lapalombara and Myron Weiner (Princeton, N.J.: Princeton University Press, 1966), chap. 5. A preliminary attempt at applying the Sartori model to the Chilean case is Rafael López Pintor, "El sístema de partidos en Chile: Un caso de pluralismo extremo," mimeographed (Santiago: INSORA, 1968). When López wrote his piece the Christian Democrats had not as yet experienced a sharp decline. He thus attributes to Chile a Center more akin to the Italian case of 1963 than to the cases of Weimar and Spain in the 1930s, where the Center was considerably weaker.

14. Sartori, "European Political Parties," pp. 156, 164.

15. For documentation of this characterisitic of the Chilean party system, see Arturo Valenzuela, *Political Brokers in Chile: Local Governemnt in a Centralized Polity* (Durham, N.C.: Duke University Press, 1977), chap. 7.

16. For a discussion of the relationship of business and government, see Constantine C. Menges, "Public Policy and Organized Buisness in Chile: A Preliminary Analysis," *Journal of International Affairs* 2, no. 2 (1966): 343–65. A thorough discussion of business confederations and professional associations can be found in David F. Cusak, "La interacción entre el sector público y los agentes mediadores en el sistema político chileno," part 2, mimeo-

graphed (Santiago: INSORA, 1968); and David F. Cusak, "The Politics of Chilean Private Enterprise under Christian Democracy," (Ph.D. diss., University of Denver, 1970).

17. On Chilean labor, see Alan Angell, *Politics and the Labour Movement in Chile* (London: Oxford University Press, 1972); Jorge Barría Serán, *Trayectoria y estructura del movimiento sindical chileno, 1946-62* (Santiago: INSORA, 1963); James O. Morris, *Elites, Intellectuals, and Consensus: A Study of the Social Question and the Industrial Relations System in Chile* (Ithaca, N.Y.: Cornell University Press, 1966); Henry Landsberger, Manuel Barrera, and Abel Toro, *El pensamiento del dirigente sindical chileno* (Santiago: INSORA, 1963); Hernán Ramírez Necochea, *Historia del movimiento obrero en Chile* (Santiago: Talleres gráficos Lautaro, 1956); Julio Samuel Valenzuela, "The Chilean Labor Movement: The Institutionalization of Conflict," in Valenzuela and Valenzuela, *Chile: Politics and Society*.

18. For documentation of these vertical linkages and the role of the legislature, see Valenzuela, *Political Brokers in Chile*, chaps. 5-7.

19. See ibid. For evolution of the system over time, see chap. 8.

20. For a detailed discussion of elements of the electoral system and reforms of 1958, see Bernaschina, *Cartilla electoral*.

21. Duncan MacRae, *Parliament, Parties, and Society in France, 1946-1958* (New York: St. Martin's Press, 1967), p. 16.

22. Alejandro Portes, "Urbanization and Politics in Latin America," *Social Science Quarterly* 52, no. 3 (December 1971): 697-720. See also his "Occupation and Lower Class Political Orientation in Chile," in Valenzuela and Valenzuela, *Chile: Politics and Society*.

23. For another discussion of Chilean voting behavior which also emphasizes some of the heterogeneous bases of support, see Robert Ayres, "Unidad Popular and the Chilean Electoral Process," in Valenzuela and Valenzuela, *Chile: Politics and Society*, pp. 30-67. It must be stressed again that the Socialists had much more heterogeneous bases of support than the Communists and relied, particularly in earlier periods, primarily on traditional clientelistic politics. For documentation, see Chelén Rojas, *Trayectoria del socialismo*.

24. Oficina de Planificación Nacional, *Plan de la economía nacional: Antecedentes sobre el desarrollo chileno, 1960-70* (Santiago: ODEPLAN, 1971), pp. 7, 170-76, 372, 383. This volume is an excellent summary of the state of the Chilean economy and the role of the public sector as of 1970. For a discussion using many of the same figures and comparative data on other Latin American countries, see Sergio Bitar, "La estructura económica chilena y la transición al socialismo," *Mensaje* 20, nos. 202-3 (September-October 1971): 404-12.

25. See the excellent study "Public Enterprises: Their Present Significance and Their Potential in Development," *Economic Bulletin for Latin America* 15, no. 2 (2d semester 1970): 1-70, for this information and information on other Latin American countries. At the same time the importance of a highly concentrated private industrial and financial sector should not be minimized. See Ricardo Lagos Escobar, *La concentración del poder económico* (Santiago: Editorial del Pacífico, 1961); and Maurice Zeitlin and Richard Ratcliff, "The Concentration of National and Foreign Capital in Chile," in Valenzuela and Valenzuela, *Chile: Politics and Society*, pp. 297-337.

26. For a definition of praetorianism and an influential discussion of political institutionalization, see Samuel P. Huntington, *Political Order in Changing Societies* (New Haven: Yale University Press, 1968), especially chap. 4.

27. For the Chilean Senate debate on this incident, see *El Mercurio*, 27 June 1969, p. 13.

28. See J. S. Valenzuela, "The Chilean Labor Movement," in Valenzuela and Valenzuela, *Chile: Politics and Society*, pp. 135-171.

29. The best single comprehensive description of Chilean institutions before the coup is Gil, *Political System of Chile*.

30. Alejandro Silva Bascuñan, *Tratado de derecho constitucional*, 3 vols. (Santiago: Editorial Jurídica, 1963).

31. For a discussion of the Contraloría, see Enrique Silva Cimma, *Derecho administrativo chileno y comparado*, 2d ed. (Santiago: Editorial Jurídica, 1969), vol. 2. According to Silva Cimma, from 1959 to 1969 Chilean presidents did not issue *decretos de insistencia* aimed at overruling the Contraloría (see p. 368). On Chilean public finances, see Hugo Araneda Dörr, *La administración financiera del estado* (Santiago: Editorial Jurídica, 1966). On municipal finances and the role of the Contraloría, see A. Valenzuela, *Political Brokers in Chile*, chap. 2.

32. Several excellent studies on the Chilean bureaucracy have appeared. These include Germán Urzúa Valenzuela and Anamaría García Barzelatto, *Diagnóstico de la burocracia chilena* (Santiago: Editorial Jurídica, 1971); Germán Urzúa Valenzuela, *Evolución de la administración pública chilena (1818–1968)* (Santiago: Editorial Jurídica, 1970); Rafael López Pintor, "Development Administration in Chile: Structural, Normative and Behavioral Constraints to Performance," (Ph.D. diss., University of North Carolina, 1972) and his *Una Explicación Sociológica del Cambio Administrativo: Chile, 1812–1970* (Madrid: Documentación Administrativa, no. 168, 1975).

33. See A. Valenzuela, *Political Brokers in Chile*, chap. 6.

34. For a discussion of some of these problems from the point of view of the planner, see Osvaldo Contreras Strauch, *Antecedentes y perspectivas de la planificación en Chile* (Santiago: Editorial Jurídica, 1971). This work was heavily influenced by the thinking of Osvaldo Sunkel.

35. See Menges, "Public Policy and Organized Business in Chile."

36. Jacques Chonchol, "Poder y reforma agraria en la experiencia chilena," in Anibal Pinto et al., *Chile Hoy* (Mexico: Siglo XXI, 1970), p. 296. According to Chonchol, when the Christian Democrats came into office agricultural policy was set by twenty-one different agencies dependent on five different ministries. As late as 1966 the Ministry of Agriculture controlled only 11 percent of agricultural credit and only 2 percent of rural investments (see pp. 303–4). This is one of the best treatments available of the complexities of the unwieldy public sector.

37. See the remarks of Carmen Lazo, a popular Socialist deputy, criticizing the excessive technocracy of the public sector during the Allende period and calling for a greater role for the non-specialist, in *Ercilla*, 11 July 1973, p. 11. See also Chonchol, "Poder y reforma agraria en la experiencia Chilena."

38. On the "praetorian" aspects of Argentine politics, see Eldon Kenworthy, "Coalitions in the Political Development of Latin America," in *The Study of Coalition Behavior: Theoretical Perspectives from Four Continents* ed. Sven Groennings, E. W. Kelley, and Michael Leiserson (New York: Holt, Rinehart and Winston, 1970), pp. 103–4. For a fascinating discussion of the "impossible" Argentine political game, see Guillermo O'Donnell, *Modernization and Bureaucratic-Authoritarianism: Studies in South American Politics* (University of California at Berkeley: Institute of International Studies, 1973), chap. 4.

39. On the Chilean Senate, see Weston Agor, *The Chilean Senate* (Austin: University of Texas Press, 1971). An invaluable study of the workings of the Chilean legislature is Jorge Tapia Valdés, *La técnica legislativa* (Santiago: Editorial Jurídica, 1960). For a discussion of the role of the legislature in Chilean politics over time, with particular emphasis on the importance of the parliamentary republic in the institutionalization of Chilean politics, see A. Valenzuela, *Political Brokers in Chile*, chap. 8.

40. This argument is developed in Arturo Valenzuela and Alexander Wilde, "Presidentialist Politics and the Decline of the Chilean Congress," in *Legislatures and Political Development*, ed. Joel Smith and Lloyd Mussolf (Durham, N.C.: Duke University Press, 1978).

41. Derived from Roman law, it means the search for a rightful redress of grievances or the obtension of rightful demands through the legal process.

42. An excellent summary and analysis of the extensive debate on Chilean inflation, which goes back into the nineteenth century, can be found in Albert O. Hirschman, *Journeys toward Progress* (New York: The Twentieth Century Fund, 1963). A classic study of earlier inflation is Frank W. Fetter, *Monetary Inflation in Chile* (Princeton, N.J.: Princeton University Press, 1931). Influential studies of Chilean inflation include Osvaldo Sunkel, "La inflación chilena: Un enfoque heterodoxo," *El Trimestre Económico* 25 (October-December 1958); Luis Escobar, "Desocupación con inflación: El caso chileno," *Panorama Económico*, August 1959; Nicolás Kaldor, "Problemas económicos de Chile," *El Trimestre Económico* 26 (April-June 1959).

43. An excellent recent study of industrialization in Chile is Henry W. Kirsh, "The Industrialization of Chile, 1880–1970," (Ph.D. diss., University of Florida, 1973). See also Oscar Muñoz, *Crecimiento industrial de Chile, 1914-1965* (Santiago: Universidad de Chile, Instituto de Economía y Planificación, 1968), p. 26. Among the many fine general treatments of the Chilean economy, see: Francisco A. Encina, *Nuestra inferioridad económica* (Santiago: Editorial Universitaria, S.A., 1955); Anibal Pinto Santa Cruz, *Chile: Un caso de*

desarrollo frustrado (Santiago: Editorial Universitaria, S.A., 1959); idem, *Chile: Una economía difícil* (México: Fondo de Cultura Económica, 1964); Ricardo Ffrench-Davis, *Políticas económicas en Chile, 1952-1970* (Santiago: Ediciones Nueva Universidad, 1973); Oscar Muñoz et al., *Proceso a la industrialización chilena* (Santiago: Centro Estudios de Planificacion Nacional, 1972); Markos Mamalakis and Clark Reynolds, eds. *Essays on the Chilean Economy* (Homewood, Ill.: Richard D. Irwin, 1964); José Cademártori, *La economía chilena* (Santiago: Editorial Universitaria, 1968).

44. Quoted in Valenzuela and Wilde, "Presidentialist Politics." Hans Daalder makes a similar argument in differentiating the political evolution of several European countries. See his "Parties, Elites and Political Developments in Western Europe," in Lapalombara and Weiner, *Political Parties and Political Development*, p. 60.

45. In the United States an ideology of "disjointed incrementalism" seems to be congruent with that of incrementalist decision-making. See Charles E. Lindbloom, *The Intelligence of a Democracy* (New York: The Free Press, 1965). On the ideology of master planning in Chile and other Latin American countries, see Hirschman's provocative analysis in *Journeys toward Progress*.

46. For historical treatments of the Chilean military, see Frederick M. Nunn, *Chilean Politics, 1920-31: The Honorable Mission of the Armed Forces* (Albuquerque: University of New Mexico Press, 1970); and idem, *The Military in Chilean History* (Albuquerque: University of New Mexico Press, 1976).

47. In a survey conducted in 1967 the overwhelming majority of respondents noted that the military did not have a political role. See Roy Allen Hansen, "Military Culture and Organizational Decline: A Study of the Chilean Army," (Ph.D. diss., University of California at Los Angeles, 1968), chap. 4. Basing his observations on a comprehensive survey of retired officers, Hansen notes that military officers picked their five best friends almost exclusively from the ranks of fellow officers.

48. This theme came through very strongly in interviews with Chilean politicians conducted by the author in 1969 and 1974. Hansen, however, notes that his population sample held the military in higher esteem on qualities such as honesty and trustworthiness than they did other elite groups, including politicians (see ibid).

49. Charles Lewis Taylor and Michael C. Hudson, *World Handbook of Political and Social Indicators* (New Haven: Yale University Press, 1972), pp. 35, 39.

50. See the works by Nunn referred to in n. 46. This point is forcefully made in a good article on the Chilean military after the coup by Jorge Neff entitled, "The Politics of Repression: The Social Pathology of the Chilean Military," in *Latin American Perspectives* 1, no. 2 (Summer 1974): 59-63. See also the work by Alain Joxe, *Las Fuerzas armadas en el sistema político de Chile* (Santiago: Editorial Universitaria, 1970).

51. Statistics for the pre-Alessandri period are from Gil, *Political System of Chile*, p. 178. The most recent statistics can be found in Dirección de Presupuestos, Ministerio de Hacienda, *Balance Consolidado del Sector Público* for relevant years.

52. See chap. 2 below.

53. *Ercilla*, 15-21 September 1965, p. 8. Cited in Arturo Valenzuela, "The Chilean Political System and the Armed Forces, 1810-1925" (M.A. thesis, Columbia University, 1967), p. 144.

54. Hansen, "Military Culture and Organizational Decline," p. 254. Thus the Chilean military conceived of their role in similar terms as the Brazilian military and the military in other Latin American countries. For a brilliant discussion of the guardian role in Brazil, see Alfred Stepan, *The Military in Politics: Changing Patterns in Brazil* (Princeton, N.J.: Princeton University Press, 1971), pt. 2.

CHAPTER 2

1. See Juan Linz, *The Breakdown of Democratic Regimes: Crisis, Breakdown, and Reequilibration* (Baltimore, Md.: Johns Hopkins University Press, 1978).

2. See the influential essay by James C. Davies, "Toward a Theory of Revolution," *American Sociological Review*, 27 (February 1962): 5-16. For a thorough review of relative depriva-

tion theories which attempt to explain political disorder and violence, see Ted Robert Gurr, *Why Men Rebel* (Princeton, N.J.: Princeton University Press, 1970).

3. For a recent and important version of this argument, see Samuel P. Huntington, *Political Order in Changing Societies* (New Haven: Yale University Press, 1968), chap. 1. See also Karl Deutsch, "Social Mobilization and Political Development," *American Political Science Review*, 55 (September 1961): 492–502.

4. For an interesting analysis which challenges Huntington's notion that weak institutionalization leads to decay and exposes some of the ambiguities of his argument, see Mark Kesselman, "Overinstitutionalization and Political Constraint: The Case of France," *Comparative Politics* 111 (October 1970): 21–44.

5. See the excellent publication by the Dirección de Presupuesto, Ministerio de Hacienda, *Balance consolidado del sector público de Chile años 1969-1970 y período 1964-1970* (Santiago: Talleres Gráficos del Servicio de Prisiones, 1973), p. 36.

6. See Martin Needler, *Political Development in Latin America* (New York: Random House, 1968), p. 90.

7. For this thesis see Almino Alffonso et al., *Movimiento campesino chileno*, 2 vols. (Santiago: ICIRA, 1970). See also Brian Loveman, "The Transformation of the Chilean Countryside," in *Chile: Politics and Society*, ed. Arturo Valenzuela and J. Samuel Valenzuela (New Brunswick, N.J.: Transaction, Inc., 1976), pp. 238–96.

8. See Mario Bernaschina, *Cartilla electoral* (Santiago: Editorial Jurídica, 1958).

9. Population figures are derived from publications of the Instituto Nacional de Estadística; all voting figures come from the Dirección del Registro Electoral, Santiago, Chile.

10. The excellent article by Landsberger and McDaniel deals primarily with the Popular Unity period. This author agrees with most of their analysis, though he interprets somewhat differently mobilization in the pre-Allende period. See "Hypermobilization in Chile, 1970–73," *World Politics* 28, no. 4 (July 1976): 538.

11. Data for 1967 from Dirección de Estadística y Censos, "Chile industria manufacturera: Número de establecimientos y ocupación en el año 1967," mimeographed, 1968, p. 8. The figures for 1957 are taken from the excellent publication by the Instituto de Economía, Universidad de Chile, *La economía de Chile en el período 1950-1963*, vol. 2 (Santiago: Instituto de Economía, 1963), p. 105. According to the Oficina de Planificación Nacional (ODEPLAN), employment in large firms tripled in the same period. See ODEPLAN, *Plan de la economía nacional Antecedentes sobre el desarrollo chileno, 1960-70* (Santiago: ODEPLAN, 1971), p. 181.

12. Interviews with the author in Santiago de Chile in October, November, and December of 1974.

13. This point is made in Alan Angell, *Politics and the Labour Movement in Chile* (London: Oxford University Press, 1972), p. 67. I am indebted to Samuel Valenzuela for his helpful comments on this section.

14. The three main campesino confederations were: Triunfo Campesino, formed initially by INDAP of the Ministry of Agriculture; Libertad, which grouped organizations connected with the church and the Christian Democratic party; and Ranquil, associated with Marxist parties. In 1969 Triunfo Campesino had almost 50 percent of the affiliates, but by late 1972 Ranquil came to predominate with about half of the unionized rural workers. Data from Dirección del Trabajo, Santiago.

15. See the sources cited in n. 7.

16. In fact, in 1920 there were as many as 270,000 unionized workers, not counting empleados. With an active population of 1,228,000, this meant that as early as that date 22 percent of the active workers were unionized. For the union figures see U.S. Bureau of Labor Statistics, *Bulletin*, no. 461 (October 1928). The figures on active population come from República de Chile, *Censo de la población de chile, 1930*, p. vii. For a revisionary work on the Chilean labor movement which analyzes these findings, see the forthcoming doctoral dissertation by J. Samuel Valenzuela, "The French and Chilean Labor Movements" (Columbia University, 1978).

17. Angell, *Politics and the Labour Movement*, p. 76. See also J. Samuel Valenzuela, "The Chilean Labor Movement: The Institutionalization of Conflict," in Valenzuela and Valenzuela, *Chile: Politics and Society*, pp. 135–71.

18. See the chapter entitled "Participación nacional y popular," in Eduardo Frei, *Cuarto mensaje presidencial*, 21 May 1968, for a discussion of the rationale behind "popular participation." See also the publications of DESAL (Centro para el Desarrollo Económico y Social de América Latina). For an evaluation of the urban effort, see Luis Alvarado, Rosemond Cheetham, and Gastón Rojas, "Mobilización social en torno al problema de la vivienda," *EURE* 3, no. 7 (April 1973): 27–70.

19. Gabriel Almond, "Popular Development: Analytical and Normative Perspectives," *Comparative Political Studies* 1, no. 4 (January 1969): 463.

20. For a good discussion of the 1964 election see Federico Gil, *The Political System of Chile* (Boston: Houghton Mifflin Co., 1966), chap. 7.

21. U.S. intervention in the 1964 election has long been the subject of discussion. For an early treatment see the study, based in part on Eastern European intelligence, by Eduardo Labarca, *Chile invadido* (Santiago: Editorial Austral, 1969), chap. 3. More precise details of the U.S. role were revealed in the staff report of the Select Committee to Study Governmental Operations with respect to United States Intelligence, *Covert Action in Chile* (Washington, D.C.: U.S. Government Printing Office, 18 December 1975), pp. 14–19. A CIA study concluded that "U.S. intervention enabled Eduardo Frei to win a clear majority in the 1964 election, instead of merely a plurality" (ibid, p. 17). Three million dollars was a tremendous amount of money in the Chilean context, amounting to $1.20 per vote. Labarca argues that the Frei campaign received close to $20 million, including money from European and private sources. As a comparison, in 1964 the Goldwater and Johnson campaigns together spent 54 cents per vote. See Congressional Quarterly, *Politics in America*, 4th ed. (Washington, D.C.: Congressional Quarterly, 1971), p. 80.

22. Between 1964 and 1969 the CIA spent $2 million in Chile, not only for electoral support but also to strengthen Christian Democratic support among peasants and slum dwellers. See *Covert Action in Chile*, pp. 17–19. It is an open secret that DESAL, the "think tank" headed by Jesuit Roger Vekemans which drew up most of the blueprints for "*promoción popular*," was supported by the CIA. Table 20 in chap. 3 provides information on the vast U.S. aid to the Frei government.

23. These observations are based on the author's research experience in Chile in 1969. The argument of this section is elaborated much more fully in Arturo Valenzuela and Alexander Wilde, "Presidentialist Politics and the Decline of the Chilean Congress," in *Legislatures and Political Developments*, ed. Joel Smith and Lloyd Mussolf (Durham, N.C.: Duke University Press, forthcoming). For a good example of the debate of the period, see the special issue on the 1967 municipal elections put out by *Ercilla*, 29 March 1967. The Christian Democrats called for an end to the "old style of give and take and the politics of the political clique" (p. 25). The vice-president of the Radical party bitterly criticized the government's attempt to turn the municipal election into a plebiscite, noting that "a long tradition has been broken as the head of state has cast himself in the role of electoral leader" (p. 3).

24. A good case study of the agrarian reform decision is Robert R. Kaufman, *The Politics of Land Reform in Chile, 1950–1970* (Cambridge, Mass.: Harvard University Press, 1972). On the copper decision, see Theodore Moran, *Multinational Corporations and the Politics of Dependence: Copper in Chile* (Princeton, N.J.: Princeton University Press, 1974).

25. The statistics cited earlier in this chapter show that the government made considerable progress in achieving its objectives. However, it was not necessary for it to adopt an arrogant attitude in attaining that end. At one point the government sought to bar congressmen from granting subsidies to local organizations, a traditional pork barrel which represented an infinitesimal portion of the budget. The consideration was one purely of "efficiency." The political ramifications only became obvious after a storm of opposition was raised. See Valenzuela and Wilde, "Presidentialist Politics and the Decline of the Chilean Congress."

26. Ibid. A thorough legislative history of the reforms can be found in Guillermo Piedrabuena Richards, *La reforma constitucional* (Santiago: Ediciones Encina, 1970). Major essays presenting the government's viewpoint on the reforms can be found in Eduardo Frei et al., *Reforma constitucional 1970* (Santiago: Editorial Jurídica, 1970).

27. The history of the MIR has yet to be written.

28. See the articles by Michael Leiserson, "Game Theory and the Study of Coalition Behavior," and E. W. Kelley, "Bargaining in Coalition Situations," in *The Study of Coalition Behavior: Theoretical Perspectives from Four Continents,* ed. Sven Groennings, E. W. Kelly, and Michael Leiserson (New York: Holt, Rinehart and Winston, 1970).
29. In understanding the potential for coalition-building before the election, it must also be stressed that the Right, in a situation unlike that of 1964, had a very viable candidate in ex-president Alessandri. The Right felt that if there were to be a Right-Center coalition again, it would have to be around their candidate this time.
30. It is also clear from the Christian Democratic Party Congress of 1969 that, despite Tomic's stand, the party was not prepared to move sharply to the left.
31. For some of the limitations of game theory in the study of politics, see Leiserson, "Game Theory and the Study of Coalition Behavior," pp. 270–72. See also the discussion by Scott C. Flanigan in *Crisis, Choice, and Change: Historical Studies of Political Development*, ed. Gabriel A. Almond, Scott C. Flanigan, and Robert C. Mundt (Boston: Little, Brown and Co., 1972), pp. 67–72.
32. For the first time in Chilean politics television was important in a presidential campaign. This clearly hurt Alessandri, who was not able to live up to his image of an austere, nonpartisan, and wise leader. He looked tired and feeble, and he overstressed the theme that workers must work more for less if the country was to prosper.
33. An excellent summary and analysis of the three presidential platforms, using categories derived from the sociology of knowledge, is Frédéric Debuyst and Joan E. Garcés, "La opción chilena de 1970: Análisis de los tres programas electorales," *Revista Latinoamericana de Ciencia Política* 2, no. 2 (August 1971): 279–369. The authors present a detailed side-by-side table of the three platforms in a lengthy Appendix.
34. Allende made this argument repeatedly in his public statements. For a concrete example, see his first speech before the joint session of Congress in Salvador Allende, *Salvador Allende: Su pensamiento político* (Santiago: Empresa Editora Nacional Quimantú Limitada, 1972), p. 112. An English translation of the speech can be found in Regis Debray, *The Chilean Revolution: Conversations with Allende* (New York: Random House, Vintage Books, 1971). The question of a revolution within the ongoing legal system led to a significant intellectual debate in Chilean circles. The foremost articulator of this view is Eduardo Novoa. See his "Vías legales para avanzar hacia el socialismo," *Mensaje*, no. 208 (April 1971), pp. 84–90, which suggests how legislation on the books, dating in some cases from the brief Socialist experiment of 1932, could be used to move legally toward a Socialist economy. The Allende administration would make use of these regulations during its term in office. For a more pessimistic appraisal of the move to socialism within legal frameworks, which stresses the constraints of the legal system, see Eduardo Novoa, "Aspectos constitucionales y legales de la política del gobierno de la Unidad Popular," in *La vía chilena al socialismo*, ed. Gabriel Palma (Mexico: Siglo XXI, 1973). For an excellent series of articles on the same topic, see the special edition on "Revolución y legalidad: Problemas del estado y el derecho en Chile," of *Cuadernos de la Realidad Nacional*, no. 15 (December 1972).
35. See his *The Breakdown of Democratic Regimes*.
36. Though Allende was identified with the more moderate faction of the party, he supported the election of Carlos Altamirano to the party leadership, in large measure because of personal rivalries and disputes. Many in the moderate faction of the party had pushed for the nomination of Aniceto Rodriguez as the presidential candidate of the Left, believing that Allende had had his chance in the past and had failed. The support for Altamirano can also be interpreted as an effort on the part of the president to regain a measure of influence over the left wing of the party. Strained relations with the leadership of his own party was to be an important feature of his government.
37. See the fascinating interview with Luis Corvalán, secretary general of the Chilean Communist party, in Eduardo Labarca, *Corvalán 27 horas* (Santiago: Quimantú, 1972), esp. pp. 109–12.
38. See the study by Debuyst and Garcés, "La opción Chilena de 1970," for a comparison of the party platforms.
39. It should be stressed that this author does not feel that the more conservative wing of the

Christian Democratic party should automatically be lumped with all other "reactionaries." Most of the leadership of this group had and has a strong commitment to democracy. They were clearly "moderates" within the Chilean context.

40. Data on the breakdown of seats in the Congress were obtained from the Oficina de Informaciones de la Cámara de Diputados and the Oficina de Informaciones del Senado.

41. Though traditionally the front-runner had been elected in the Congress, this does not mean that parties supporting the runner-up in the popular election also voted for the front-runner; they usually voted for their own candidate. Thus in 1946 the Conservatives voted for Eduardo Cruz-Coke, in 1952 the Radicals voted for Pedro Alfonso, and in 1958 the FRAP voted for Allende. In 1970 the Christian Democrats found themselves in the peculiar position of commanding the key block of votes in the Congress but having no presidential candidate in contention.

42. For an analysis of U.S. action see the interim report of the Select Committee to Study Governmental Operations with respect to intelligence activities, United States Senate, *Alleged Assassination Plots Involving Foreign Leaders* (Washington, D.C.: U.S. Government Printing Office, 20 November 1975), pp. 225–54. The lengths to which the Central Intelligence Agency went is illustrated by Cable 882, Headquarters to Station, 10/19/70, in which the station was urged to fabricate a justification for a coup. Suggestions included the use of "firm" intelligence that Cubans would reorganize intelligence services along Soviet-Cuban lines and that Allende planned to empty armories to the Communist Peoples' Militia. Station noted that "we are now asking you to prepare intel report based on some well-known facts and some fiction to justify coup, split opposition, and gain adherents for military coup. With appropriate military contact can determine how to 'discover' intel report which could even be planted during raids planned by Carabineros [quotation marks in original]." See p. 234. Nixon himself initiated the action in a meeting that took place on 15 September 1970 with Henry Kissinger, National Security Council adviser; John Mitchell, attorney general; and Richard Helms, director of the Central Intelligence Agency. The president noted that $10 million could be spent on the operation, that the Chilean economy should be made to "scream," and that every effort should be made to "Save Chile" (p. 227). Though the embassy was not involved in the kidnapping plot, Ambassador Korry put great pressure on Frei to stop Allende's bid for the presidency. In a situation report the ambassador noted that he had sent a message to Frei to the effect that "Frei should know that not a nut or bolt will be allowed to reach Chile under Allende. Once Allende comes to power we shall do all within our power to condemn Chile and the Chileans to utmost deprivation and poverty, a policy designed for a long time to come to accelerate the hard features of a Communist society in Chile" (p. 231).

43. See Daniel Levine, "The Role of Political Learning in the Restoration and Consolidation of Democracy: Venezuela since 1958," in Linz and Stepan, *The Breakdown of Democratic Regimes*, vol. 3, *The Problem in the Latin American Context*.

CHAPTER 3

1. The program of the Popular Unity government has been published in Gabriel Palma, *La vía chilena al socialismo* (Mexico: Siglo XXI, 1973), pp. 269–92. The same book includes the platform of the Popular Unity drawn up for the 1973 congressional elections (see pp. 293–322). For an English translation, see Ann Zammit, ed., *The Chilean Way to Socialism* (Austin: The University of Texas Press, 1973).

2. Events referred to in this study were widely reported in the Chilean press. The author relied primarily on *El Mercurio Edición Internacional, Ercilla, Chile Hoy,* and the British periodical *Latin America* for the general chronology. For more in-depth study of important events, such as the conversations of mid-1972 between the government and the Christian Democrats, the daily press was used, including *El Mercurio, La Nación, La Prensa, El Siglo, Las Noticias de Ultima Hora, Mayoría,* and other newspapers. Though *El Mercurio* is an extremely conservative paper and sought from the outset to destroy the Allende government, it was and is the primary newspaper of record, reporting the full texts of statements made by parties and

leaders, and printing official statistics, documents, and Senate debates. Material from interviews with key political actors helped supplement published sources.

3. See Regis Debray, *The Chilean Revolution: Conversations with Allende* (New York: Random House, Vintage Books, 1971).

4. For a general statement of the government economic policy, see the presentation made by the minister of economics, Pedro Vuskovic, in October 1971 and published in Lelio Basso et al., *Transición al socialismo y experiencia chilena* (Santiago: CESO-CEREN, 1972), pp. 99–114. A clear statement of Popular Unity policy, stressing primarily economic factors such as the importance of increased demand to offset idle plant capacity, can be found in Julio López, "La estrategia económica del gobierno de la Unidad Popular," *Cuadernos de la Realidad Nacional*, no. 9 (September 1971), pp. 69–86.

5. Basso et al., *Transición al socialismo*, pp. 101–2. In a seminar held in March 1972, when the economic situation had deteriorated considerably, Vuskovic stressed much more strongly these political goals as the primary criteria for economic policy. See his "La política económica del gobierno de la Unidad Popular," in Palma, *La vía chilena al socialismo*, p. 44. See also the "debate" on pp. 79–99.

6. Stefan de Vylder, *Allende's Chile: The Political Economy of the Rise and Fall of the Unidad Popular* (Cambridge : Cambridge University Press, 1976), p. 54.

7. Ibid.

8. On the money supply see table 24.

9. De Vylder, *Allende's Chile*, p. 63. Allende summarized the first year's economic accomplishments in his message of 4 November 1971. See *Allende: Su pensamiento político*, pp. 260–61, 266–67.

10. Ibid., pp. 70–71.

11. During the first six months of 1971 inflation was 11.1 percent, still very favorable as compared to the last year of the Frei administration, when inflation had reached 34.9 percent. These figures from the Instituto Nacional de Estadística are printed in *Oficina de Informaciones del Senado, Boletín Informativo Económico*, 16 June 1972, p. 1.

12. See the works of Eduardo Novoa, cited chap. 2, no. 34. See also part 4 of Andrés Echeverría and Luis Frei, *La lucha por la juricidad en Chile* (Santiago: Editorial del Pacífico, 1974), vol. 1, for reprints of several additional articles by Novoa, and the declaration of Minister of Economics Orlando Millas and the Comptroller General Héctor Humeres on the "resquicios legales."

13. De Vylder, *Allende's Chile*, p. 145.

14. Most U.S. firms were nationalized with no dispute. This was the case, for example, with RCA Victor, Bethlehem Steel, and all the U.S. bank offices in Chile. There were difficulties with other companies such as ITT and the Ford Motor Company. The Ford plant was accused of illegally shutting down operations and of cutting off the importation of vital parts. It was taken over by workers, and eventually the government intervened. See *El Mercurio Edición Internacional*, 31 May–6 June 1971, p. 8. The ITT became notorious for its attempts to stop Allende's election by urging economic sabotage and attempting to enlist U.S. intelligence in its efforts. ITT's role was first exposed by columnist Jack Anderson in the *Washington Post*, 22 March 1972, p. C23. The ITT documents, incriminating the company in a blatant conspiracy to meddle in Chilean affairs, were published in *Documentos secretos de la ITT* (Santiago: Empresa Editoral Nacional Quimantú, 1972). For further information see the Report to the Committee on Foreign Relations, United States Senate, by the Subcommittee on Multinational Corporations, "The International Telephone and Telegraph Company and Chile, 1970–71," 21 June 1973 (Washington, D.C.: Government Printing Office, 1973).

15. See the speech by Jacques Chonchol, *El Mercurio Edición Internacional*, 15–21 February 1971, p. 6. Page 1 of the same issue reports on sharp exchanges in the Chilean Senate over the issue of violence and expropriations in the countryside. It also contains a statement made by the six leaders of the Popular Unity parties asserting the government's commitment to carry out the agrarian reform process within the law.

16. *Allende: Su pensamiento político*, p. 256.

17. In studying Chilean elections, care must be taken not to compare elections for different offices. Elections for local office so often revolve around local issues and candidates that it is

122   ARTURO VALENZUELA

misleading to compare them with senatorial and presidential elections. Elections for the Chamber of Deputies often combine local and national issues. For a discussion of local campaigning, see Arturo Valenzuela, *Political Brokers in Chile: Local Government in a Centralized Polity* (Durham, N.C.: Duke University Press, 1977), chap. 4.

18. Basso et al., *Transición al socialismo*, p. 107.
19. De Vylder, *Allende's Chile*, p. 66.
20. See *El Mercurio Edición Internacional*, 28 May–3 June 1972, p. 2.
21. These data come from the Superintendencia de Aduanas and the Banco Central, *El Mercurio Edición Internacional*, 23–29 August 1971, p. 2. According to figures projected by the Sociedad de Fomento Fabril, by 1973 food imports would account for 75 percent of copper earnings. See *El Mercurio Edición Internacional*, 30 July–5 August 1973, p. 2. Much of the problem stemmed from the fact that increased demand was not channeled into economic sectors with idle capacity, such as the durable goods industry, but was directed into areas, such as agriculture, that were already incapable of meeting demand. The policy of increasing the wages of working-class elements was simply not conducive to bailing out a consumer-goods-oriented industry that was lagging. For an economic analysis along these lines see *El Mercurio Edición Internacional*, 7–13 June 1971, p. 2. These difficulties were recognized by government economists like López. See his "La estrategia económica."
22. Basso et al. *Transición al socialismo*, p. 107.
23. See n. 21 for the source of these data.
24. *El Mercurio Edición Internacional*, 24–30 July 1972, p. 2.
25. For documentation of the U.S. blockade, see Elizabeth Farnsworth, Richard Feinberg, and Eric Leeson, "The Invisible Blockade: The United States Reacts," in *Chile: Politics and Society*, ed. Arturo Valenzuela and J. Samuel Valenzuela (New Brunswick, N.J.: Transaction, Inc., 1976), pp. 338–73. For a statement by a Chilean official on the rationale behind U.S. policy, see Armando Uribe, *Le livre noir de l'intervention américaine au Chile* (Paris: Editions du Seuil, 1974). Uribe notes that Chilean policy-makers felt that the United States was less concerned about the copper nationalization than the impact a successful Allende experiment might have on the internal politics of France and Italy. The election of leftist governments in those countries would affect the balance of forces between East and West. This view was expressed by Henry Kissinger in a "deep background briefing" (see Uribe, *Le livre noir*, pp. 92–93, 202). It is quite probable that the U.S. State Department was more concerned with Allende's "Communist" policies and his treatment of foreign capital than Kissinger's office was. However, Kissinger's office had largely taken over the foreign policy role of the U.S. government. For documentation of the U.S. role in undermining the Chilean government both through open and covert actions, see the staff report of the Select Committee to Study Governmental Operations with Respect to Intelligence Activities, U. S., Senate, "Covert Action in Chile, 1963–73."
26. U.S., Senate, "Covert Action in Chile, 1963–73," p. 32.
27. De Vylder, *Allende's Chile*, p. 129.
28. The debate over the U.S. blockade has become extensive. Paul Sigmund, by taking the statements of U.S. officials too literally, downplayed the negative effects of the blockade in his "The 'Invisible Blockade' and the Overthrow of Allende," *Foreign Affairs* 52, no. 2 (January 1974): 322–40. For a response to Sigmund see Elizabeth Farnworth's "More Than Admitted," *Foreign Policy*, no. 16 (Fall 1974), pp. 127–41. For Sigmund's rebuttal see his "Less Than Charged," in idem, pp. 142–56. Sigmund's view was also taken to task in Richard Fagen's excellent article "The United States and Chile: Roots and Branches," *Foreign Affairs* 53, no. 2 (January 1975): 297–313. The revelations of the U.S. Senate Select Committee on Intelligence have substantially clarified the U.S. government's concerted attempts to undermine the Popular Unity government.
29. See Echeverría and Frei, *La lucha por la juricidad en Chile*, vol. 3, pt. 2, for the text of the opposition measure and other documents pertaining to its debate.
30. See Juan Linz, *The Breakdown of Democratic Regimes: Crisis, Breakdown, and Reequilibration* (Baltimore, Md.: Johns Hopkins University Press, 1978).
31. Figures from de Vylder, *Allende's Chile*, p. 91. Reajustes for various groups were widely reported in the press during this period.
32. De Vylder, *Allende's Chile*, p. 91. See the article by Andy Zimbalist and Barbara Stallings,

"Showdown in Chile," *Monthly Review* 25, no. 5 (October 1973): 1–24, which stresses the failure to instill a spirit of sacrifice in the workers. They note the efforts of the government to "demobilize" the workers and stress economic gains as the principal strategy. The Socialist party continually stressed the need to maintain and expand mobilization, and criticized the fact that the Popular Unity parties let the Committees of the Popular Unity, which had worked during the campaign, lapse. For example, see the internal party document published in *El Mercurio Edición Internacional*, 13–19 March 1972, p. 5. It is not so clear, however, as Zimbalist and Stallings maintain, that the Communists were the primary force behind the redistributive policy (p. 11). The Socialists continued to support Vuskovic, the primary architect of that policy. The Communists did frown on "mobilization" and expressed concern that the capitalist rules should not be abandoned too quickly while the economy was still essentially capitalist. See for example, Luis Corvalán's comments in Eduardo Labarca, *Corvalán 27 horas* (Santiago: Quimantú, 1972), pp. 26–27. But it is not clear to the author that, if a policy of more rapid mobilization of the masses had been instituted, the Popular Unity could have in fact deviated from a redistributive pattern. To instill notions of economic sacrifice, moral as opposed to economic incentives, would take a long period of time— longer than a six-year presidential term. Further mobilization would probably have heightened the pressure for redistribution, further aggravating the economic situation. Economic policies took effect immediately. Political policies, which some policy-makers thought should accompany economic policies, would have, even in the best of circumstances, taken much longer.

33. *El Mercurio Edición Internacional*, 31 January–6 February 1972, p. 5. A long document from the PIR, stating its position, is reproduced in this issue. It should be noted that the visit of Fidel Castro to Chile in late 1971 undoubtedly had a negative impact on the middle class's perception of the Allende government. Castro stayed in Chile from 10 November to 4 December 1971, and his every move was widely reported. For a compilation of Castro's speeches and press conferences see *Fidel en Chile* (Santiago: Quimantú, 1972).

34. De Vylder, *Allende's Chile*, p. 99.

35. This section is drawn primarily from extensive interviews in Santiago in August 1974 with former high-ranking officials of the Budget Bureau who served during the Allende years.

36. See *Posición*, 4 July 1972, p. 12. Allende sharply attacked these practices. See *Allende: Su pensamiento político*, p. 274.

37. Press conference reported in *El Mercurio Edición Internacional*, 2–8 August 1971, p. 1.

38. *El Mercurio Edición Internacional*, 13–19 March 1972, p. 5. See the same page for Socialist party critiques of the partisan competitiveness between Popular Unity parties. Internal criticism was brought out in several Popular Unity meetings. Important meetings took place in El Arrayán in March of 1972 and Lo Curro in June 1972.

39. For a discussion of Allende's continual exhortations to end labor indiscipline and a review of these problems, see Henry Landsberger and Tim McDaniel, "Hypermobilization in Chile, 1970–73," *World Politics* 28, no. 4 (July 1976): 502–43.

40. *El Mercurio Edición Internacional*, 31 January–6 February 1972, p. 6.

41. For the position of the MIR, see its newspaper, *El Rebelde*. A prestigious magazine of opinion, *Punto Final*, often expressed views close to those of the MIR. The official paper of the Communist party was *El Siglo*, though the party had several other publications, including, for example, *Ramona*, for more popular consumption. The leading Socialist newspaper was *Las Noticias de Ultima Hora*. In addition, weeklies such as *Mayoría* and the first-rate *Chile Hoy* presented views generally in line with those of the Socialist party. *Clarín* and *Puro Chile*, sensationalist tabloids, also supported the government. The official newspaper of the government was *La Nación*.

It should be stressed that the leadership of the Left was not necessarily very close. A very revealing fact is that the secretary general of the Communist party, Luis Corvalán, and Salvador Allende, colleagues in numerous struggles, did not use the familiar "tu" in addressing each other. Also, Communist leaders, in particular, did not often mix with leaders of other leftist parties socially. See Labarca, *Corvalán 27 horas*, p. 199. Corvalán also notes that the rivalries between followers were particularly intense (p. 198).

42. From the *Manifiesto de Concepción* issued on 22 May 1972 and reprinted in several newspapers. For a summary, see *El Mercurio Edición Internacional*, 22–28 May 1972, p. 1.

43. See the transcript of his press conference in *El Mercurio*, 27 May 1972, p. 25. For Allende's criticism of the ultra-leftists, see *Allende: Su pensamiento político*, pp. 211–12.
44. *El Mercurio Edición Internacional*, 9–15 August 1971, p. 5.
45. See Debray, *Chilean Revolution*, especially pp. 72–77.
46. *El Mercurio*, 27 May 1972, p. 25.
47. It must be stressed that much of the violence was blown out of proportion in the press accounts. Large headlines and shrill radio and television accounts conveyed the impression that what had been an isolated incident of violence had engulfed the whole nation. It is clear that with the relaxation of government violence and increased mobilization Chile was facing a level of confrontation not seen since the turbulent 1930s. But the perception of violence no doubt exceeded the real dimensions of violence, thereby having an exaggerated political impact.
48. The position of the Right was amply presented in the media. For the position of the far Right, including Patria y Libertad, see *Tribuna*, *Sepa*, and *PEC*. *El Mercurio*, which moved increasingly to the disloyal opposition and became a principal mouthpiece for the arch-conservative tendencies of the military junta after the coup, often printed ads for the extreme rightist group. See, for example, the full-page ad placed by Patria y Libertad presenting its platform and plan of action in the edition of 17 June 1972, p. 29. The *El Mercurio* company also published other dailies, such as *La Segunda*. *Qué Pasa*, a very informative conservative weekly, began to make inroads on *Ercilla*'s preeminent position in that market. The often inflammatory headlines and accounts of the Right are documented in part in Michele Mattelart and Mabel Piccine, "La prensa burguesa, no sería más que un tigre de papel?" *Cuadernos de la Realidad Nacional*, no. 16 (April 1973), pp. 250–63. As will be noted below, inflammatory headlines from both sides helped to confuse and polarize the political atmosphere.
49. The major Christian Democratic organ was *La Prensa*. As noted earlier, the popular weekly *Ercilla* also had a Christian Democratic orientation. For a moderate and leftist pro-Christian Democratic view, consult *Mensaje*. For a more conservative magazine, see the official *Política y Espíritu*.
50. For his statement, see *El Mercurio Edición Internacional*, 27 September–3 October 1971, p. 1. For a very valuable collection of documents that summarize the views of the Christian Democrats and the opposition by early 1972, see Joan E. Garcés, *Revolución, congreso, y constitución: El caso Tohá* (Santiago: Quimantú, 1972). The book reviews the movement of the Christian Democratic party away from its tentative support for the government and toward its alliance with the Right, culminating in the first successful impeachment vote, that of Allende's minister of the interior, José Tohá.
51. Actually, Christian Democrats had approached the government even earlier with a proposition that the competition between the two groups be kept at a minimum during the 1971 municipal elections. The Christian Democrats wanted to conserve their strength while not attacking the government. The government rejected the overture. The success of the Socialists in the 1971 election gave them electoral reasons (in addition to ideological objections) to striking an alliance with the Christian Democrats. As noted earlier, the Socialists gained strength dramatically to become Chile's first party. Under such circumstances Socialists could understandably perceive the Christian Democratic overtures as self-serving—at least in electoral terms. However, it is clear to this author that elements in the progressive wing of the Christian Democrats were genuinely concerned about the costs of electoral confrontation with the government and foresaw the increasing dangers of further polarization. Much of this analysis is based on interviews with high-level political leaders, primarily Christian Democrats, in Santiago, Chile, during the months of January and February of 1974. Subsequent interviews later that year corroborated the earlier ones.
52. The section of the constitution, adopted in 1970, that dealt with the question of how amendments were to be promulgated, was indeed ambiguous. According to Article 108, paragraph 1, constitutional reforms must follow the same procedures as those followed to adopt an ordinary law, with a few exceptions. The article then proceeds to note that for the adoption of an amendment, an absolute majority of members of both houses must approve the measure on two different occasions. The president cannot reject the bill submitted to him by the joint session of Congress. He can only propose modifications and corrections or

elaborate on items which he had proposed. The last paragraph states that if the president's proposals are accepted by a majority of the Congress, as specified in the second paragraph (that is, an absolute majority), the measure can then be returned to the president for promulgation. The problem is that the last paragraph does not say what happens when the Congress does not approve of the presidential modifications. According to Allende, since the first paragraph says that unless specified otherwise, a constitutional amendment follows the procedures of a simple law, and a simple law requires a two-thirds vote by the Congress in order to override presidential suggestions, a two-thirds vote was required. The president argued that the last paragraph, specifying an absolute majority of the Congress, was inserted in order to insure that a constitutional amendment could not be approved by only a majority of members present, as the constitution specifies for an ordinary law. But this requirement did not mean that the regular procedure requiring a two-thirds vote to override presidential vetoes was waived. The opposition in turn argued that the last paragraph implied not only that an absolute majority was needed to approve presidential vetoes, but that it also meant that by a mere majority the Congress could reject presidential vetoes. As far as the opposition was concerned, the last paragraph was included in Article 108 not only to specify that an absolute majority of Congress is needed for approval, but also to abolish the requirement for the two-thirds vote for overriding presidential modifications. This author, while recognizing the ambiguity, is inclined to think that the president's position was more tenable. The article clearly states that all procedures applied to a simple law must be followed, with specific exceptions. Since the exceptions do not include any reference to procedures for overriding presidential vetoes, merely a modification of the kind of majority needed to ratify those vetoes, all of the procedures for adopting a simple law should be followed. This position is shared by Alejandro Silva Bascuñan in a book published before the controversy. Silva was a prominent member of the opposition. See his "El tribunal constitucional," in Gustavo Lagos et al., *Reforma constitucional 1970* (Santiago: Editorial Jurídica, 1970), p. 262. For the constitutional reform and its legislative history, see Guillermo Piedrabuena Richards, *La reforma constitucional* (Santiago: Ediciones Encina, 1970). Piedrabuena argues that the spirit of the 1970 reforms, which provided for a plebiscite to resolve executive-legislative disputes, suggests that the impasse must be between the president and a majority, not a two-thirds majority of Congress (p. 129). This is a compelling argument, and quite logical, though it does not solve the ambiguity in the text. The Constitutional Tribunal set up to resolve such questions would in June 1973 refuse to clear up the matter. Finally, it must be added that Allende probably exceeded the provisions of Article 108 in his vetoes of the measure, which amounted to an outright rejection of many provisions of the proposed amendment. For an article supporting the position of the opposition, see Jaime Navarrete's "Observaciones del Presidente de la República y reforma constitucional," in *El Mercurio*, 28 March 1972. For an article supporting the president, see Julio Silva Solar, "Diputado Julio Silva demuestra legalidad de tesis presidencial," in *La Nación*, 17 April 1972.

53. For a compilation of documents on these talks, see Oficina de Informaciones del Senado, "Reforma constitucional que crea áreas de la economía nacional," *Boletín de Informaciones General*, no. 99, 17 April 1972.

54. Cited in *Las Noticias de Ultima Hora*, 30 June 1972, p. 4.

55. Ibid. For the position of the Communist party and the Socialist party at this time, see the articles in *Mayoría* 1, no. 37 (28 June 1972): 10–13.

56. *La Prensa*, 25 June 1972.

57. See *PEC*, 30 June 1972, p. 3. The strong feelings are reflected in some remarks which Sergio Onofre Jarpa, the president of the National party, made to Tomás Pablo, a Christian Democratic senator, in a hallway of the Senate. They are reported in *El Mercurio*, 15 June 1972, p. 15.

58. *Ercilla*, 16–22 June 1972, p. 17. The gremios flooded the papers with ads opposing talks. For an example, see *El Mercurio*, 16 June 1972, p. 17. For a good statement of the views of a powerful gremio, see the extensive report presented by Jorge Fontaine, the president of the Confederación de la Producción y del Comercio to the organization's national congress on 6 July 1972. The statement, endorsed unanimously, stresses the importance to the gremios of defending their own position and, by implication, relying less on the traditional party machinery. See *La Prensa*, 8 July 1972, pp. 6, 18.

126   ARTURO VALENZUELA

59. For a valuable discussion of these topics, noting how close the negotiations were after the first round of talks, see the interview with José Antonio Viera-Gallo, assistant secretary in the Department of Justice, published in *La Prensa*, 26 March 1972. The letters and exchanges between the government and the Christian Democrats in July were made public by Jorge Tapia, the minister of justice. The author is grateful to Jorge Tapia for providing him with the summary of the principal themes and for giving him his personal observations on the progress of the talks. In addition to other interviews with people knowledgeable about the negotiations, the author benefited greatly from attending the debates in the Chilean Congress, and particularly the Senate, during this period.

60. *Las Noticias de Ultima Hora*, 30 June 1972, p. 20. For the Christian Democratic statement on the conclusion of the talks, see *La Prensa*, 30 June 1973, p. 20.

61. In fact, in an interview with the author in 1974, a prominent Christian Democratic leader noted that Allende won considerable mileage as a result of the "weakness" of the party leadership.

62. Labarca, *Corvalán 27 horas*, p. 44.

63. For an influential discussion of Latin American politics which elaborates on the concept of "power capability," see Charles Anderson, *Politics and Economic Development in Latin America* (Englewood Cliffs, N.J.: Van Nostrand, 1967), chap. 4.

64. For an excellent discussion focusing on the confrontation dimension see David Cusak, "Confrontation Politics and the Disintegration of Chilean Democracy," *Vierteljahresberichte*, no. 58 (December 1974), pp. 313–53.

65. There is no question that the strengthening of these groups as independent entities capable of independent action was aided by contributions from foreign and domestic business circles and from U.S. intelligence. In fact, shortly before the October strikes, $24,000 was provided to an anti-Allende business organization by the CIA. In all, $8 million was spent covertly in Chile between 1970 and 1973 with over $3 million spent in fiscal 1972 alone. See U.S., Senate, "Covert Action in Chile," pp. 1, 60.

66. Several organizations did very interesting research on the popular movement in Chile during the Allende government. The best work was done on the *poblaciones*. For a sampling, see the articles by CIDU researchers Manuel Castells, Luis Alvarado, Rosemond Cheetham, Adriana Garat, Gastón Rojas, Santiago Quevedo, Eder Sader, Jorge Fiori, and Ignacio Santa Maria in vol. 3, no. 7 (April 1973) of the journal *EURE*. See also the article by the Equipo de Estudios Poblacionales del CIDU, "Reivindicación urbana y lucha política: Los campamentos de pobladores en Santiago de Chile," *EURE* 2, no. 6 (November 1972): 55–81. Another project deserving mention is the CIDU work on popular justice. See Rosemond Cheetham et al., *Pobladores: Del legalismo a la justicia popular*, 2 vols. (Santiago: CIDU, 1972).

67. Much of the literature cited in n. 66 underscores the economic orientation of the working class. In particular see Manuel Castells, "Movimiento de pobladores y lucha de clases," and Jorge Fiori, "Campamento Nueva Habana: Estudio de una experiencia de autoadministración de Justicia," both in *EURE* 3, no. 7 (April 1973). The campamento Nueva Habana was the most prominent *población* under the influence of the MIR. Even there, concerns with clientelistic matters were important, and, as Fiori notes, militancy subsided as *pobladores* began to see the Popular Unity government as the revolution already arrived. The "reivindicationist" orientation of the working class during the Popular Unity period is also strongly stressed by J. Samuel Valenzuela, "The Chilean Labor Movement: The Institutionalization of Conflict," and James Petras, "Nationalization, Socioeconomic Change, and Popular Participation," both in Valenzuela and Valenzuela, *Chile: Politics and Society*. For the best treatment yet on the role of the miners in the Allende government, which also strongly emphasizes "clientelistic" as opposed to revolutionary behavior, see Francisco Zapata, "Los mineros de Chuquicamata: Productores o proletarios?" (Mexico: Centro de Estudios Sociológicos, El Colegio de Mexico, Cuaderno no. 13, 1975). Since the miners had always constituted the backbone of support for the Left, their position was critical. Zapata shows that they continued to press for bread and butter issues as they had done when the Left was in opposition. (See n. 28, chap. 4.) The cordones formed during the October strike never really became strong enough to channel a mass movement. (On this point, see n. 58, chap. 4.) Earlier work by Henry Landsberger and his associates made similar points. See especially

Henry Landsberger, Manuel Barrera, and Abel Toro, "The Chilean Labor Union Leader: A Preliminary Report on His Background and Attitudes," *Industrial and Labor Relations Review* 17, no. 3 (April 1964): 399–420.
68. Radomiro Tomic, for one, expressed this view in an interparty memorandum, dated 7 November 1973, analyzing the situation after the coup. The opposition press, particularly the influential *El Mercurio*, received substantial covert funds from the United States to support its relentless campaign against the government. Every incident was magnified by a newspaper which reached every corner of the country. See U.S., Senate, "Covert Action," pp. 59–60. In evaluating the role of the media the author benefited from the views of several individuals. Particularly helpful were the views of a person who served in high editorial positions, including that of acting editor, of one of the most important Socialist newspapers.
69. See table 19.

CHAPTER 4

1. See Juan Linz, *The Breakdown of Democratic Regimes: Crisis, Breakdown, and Reequilibration* (Baltimore, Md.: Johns Hopkins University Press, 1978).
2. See the article "Revolucionario o Momio," in *El Mercurio Edición Internacional*, 13–19 March 1971. See also the statement of Contraloría objecting to procedures of the Dirección de Industria y Comercio (DIRINCO) in *La lucha por la juricidad en Chile*, ed. Andrés Echeverría and Luis Frei (Santiago: Editorial del Pacífico, 1974), vol. 1, pp, 311–12.
3. More broadly, the court argued that all it could do was enforce the law, and that if policy changes were sought, it was up to the legislature to modify the law. The government retorted that the court was selective in applying the law, which had considerable room for intepretation. In particular the government criticized the court's zeal in protecting private property and its refusal to curb the most libelous and seditious attacks of the opposition media. For a fascinating exchange of letters which reveals how the same "legality" was approached from different perspectives, see the exchange of letters between the president and the Supreme Court. They are reproduced in Echeverría and Frei, *La lucha por la juricidad*, vol. 3, pp. 168–98.
4. Whereas the percentage of the national budget devoted to military affairs had dropped to 5.3 percent during the Frei period (see chapter 1), it increased to 9.12 percent during the Allende years. At the same time, the government welcomed a continuation of military aid from the United States. While economic aid was reduced sharply, military aid was maintained, as the following table, showing U.S. military assistance to Chile, indicates.

Year	Military Assistance	Military Sales	Military Personnel Trained in Panama
1966	8,366,000	1,490,000	68
1967	4,766,000	1,690,000	57
1968	7,507,000	2,100,000	169
1969	2,662,000	2,147,000	107
1970	1,966,000	9,450,000	181
1971	1,033,000	2,958,000	146
1972	2,227,000	4,583,000	197
1973	918,000	2,242,000	257

SOURCE: United States, Senate, *Hearings before the Select Committee to Study Governmental Operations with Respect to Intelligence Activities*, 94th Cong., 1st sess., 4 and 5 December 1975, pp. 184–85.

5. For a revealing example of the constant effort of leaders on both sides to court the military,

and thus pressure it to subscribe to their own position, see the Senate debate of 26 October 1972, published in *El Mercurio*, 30 October 1972, p. 9.

6. The Unión Socialista Popular, the splinter party of the Socialists, did run candidates on a separate list, but they obtained only 1.6 percent of the vote. It must be stressed that the confederations were for electoral purposes only. Each of the parties continued to run the campaign as a separate organization and, as will be seen below, not without some conflict.

7. The pressure on the Christian Democrats to continue to oppose the government was revealed during the campaign by a sharp attack on party members whom the Nationals said were engaged in "secret talks" with the government to arrange for a common strategy after the election. This pressure was aimed at keeping the progressive wing of the party in line. See the declaration of the acting president of the National party, Carlos Raymond, reported in *La Prensa*, 15 February 1973. This and subsequent citations to the press in this section on the campaign are taken from the thorough step-by-step description of the public debate found in Carmen Barros and Patricio Chaparro, "La campaña de las elecciones de 1973: Chile un estudio de caso," mimeographed (Santiago: Instituto de Ciencias Políticas Universidad Católica, Documento de Trabajo No. 4, June 1974).

8. The Forty Committee, charged with overseeing U.S. covert actions, approved $1,626,666 for support of opposition candidates. See Select Committee on Intelligence, U.S., Senate, "Covert Action in Chile," p. 60. It should be reiterated that the funds went a long way, given the enormous differential between the official and the black market rate for dollars. At one time the official rate was around 40 escudos to the dollar and the black market rate 3000 to the dollar. The author interviewed one, not very prominent, congressman of the Democracia Radical party who received more money for the 1973 campaign than he had received for all previous campaigns put together. Though he was not told where the funds came from, he knew the money came from foreign sources.

9. See, for example, the interview with National party Senate candidate Fernando Ochagavía, *La Tercera de la Hora*, 9 December 1973. For the Christian Democrats see the document of the plenary council of the party, reported in *La Prensa*, 5 December 1972, and the statement of former-president Eduardo Frei, a Senate candidate for the Christian Democrats, in his declaration of candidacy speech, *La Prensa*, 5 December 1972. See also the declaration of Osvaldo Olguín, acting president of the Christian Democrats, reported in *La Prensa*, 14 February 1973. For other similar citations, see Barros and Chaparro, *La campaña de las elecciones*, pp. 59, 88.

10. See Barros and Chaparro, pp. 60–88 and 89–108.

11. For instance, see the speech by the president of the Nationals, Sergio Onofre Jarpa, published in *La Tercera de la Hora*, 14 December 1972.

12. This was a minority position in the Christian Democratic party. Among those who argued this line was Senate candidate Alejandro Noemi. See *La Tercera de la Hora*, 6 January 1973.

13. On the need for victory, see the declaration of the political commission of Patria y Libertad in *Patria y Libertad*, no. 30 (16 November 1972), p. 4. In that same issue, however, the rightist movement argued that the elections would not resolve the question because the Left only respected the force of arms (see p. 16). The utter contempt of Patria y Libertad for "liberal democracy" can be seen in the article in *Patria y Libertad*, no. 37 (4 January 1973), p. 2. These citations are drawn from Barros and Chaparro, pp. 190–92.

14. See the speech the president of the Popular Unity coalition, Senator Rafael Agustín Gumucio, published in *El Siglo*, 6 February 1973. The coalition's platform for the elections can be found in *La Nación*, 6 February 1973.

15. On the need for an alliance with the middle class and workers of other parties, see the speeches of the principal ideologue of the Communist party, Senator Volodia Teitelboim, in *El Siglo*, 30 January 1973 and 2 February 1973. For the injunction against civil war, see the speech by the secretary general of the party, Luis Corvalán, in *El Siglo*, 23 February 1973. See Barros and Chaparro, pp. 121–40.

16. See the well-publicized public letter by Carlos Altamirano published in *La Nacion*, 3 February 1973, condemning the Millas proposal.

17. For example, see the argument of Senator Carrera in *La Nación*, 3 February 1973. The position of the Socialists can be found in Carlos Altamirano, *Tres documentos* (Santiago: Ediciones SCI, 1973), and in Barros and Chaparro, pp. 141–60.

18. For the MAPU, see the electoral platform published in *La Nación*, 4 February 1973, and the declaration of Oscar Guillermo Garretón in *Revista de Frente*, no. 14 (1–15 November 1972). On the MIR position, which held that the elections were simply an artifact of the bourgeoisie and the dominant classes and were consequently a poor arena for confrontation, see the exchange of letters with the Socialist party published in *Punto Final*, no. 176 (30 January 1973), p. 2. On the need to accelerate confrontation, see the two articles by Manuel Cabieses, "Cambia el Gobierno si pierde en marzo," *Punto Final*, no. 174 (2 January 1973), p. 3; and "El dilema de marzo: avanzar o transar," *Punto Final*, no. 178 (27 February 1973), p. 2.
19. *Ercilla*, 14–20 March 1973.
20. *Ercilla*, 4–10 April 1973.
21. *Ercilla*, 11–17 April 1973, p. 10.
22. The controversy over the ENU was widely reported in the press.
23. This section is based on interviews.
24. The church's declaration on the controversy and the answer of the minister of education can be found in Carlos Oviedo, ed., *Documentos del episcopado: Chile 1970–73* (Santiago: Ediciones Mundo, 1974), pp. 151–58.
25. *Ercilla*, 18–24 April 1973, p. 13.
26. *Ercilla*, 25 April–1 May 1973, p. 8.
27. *Ercilla*, 25–31 May 1973, p. 13.
28. The El Teniente strike was a severe blow to the government at a time when it needed more than ever to project an image of unified working-class support. The strike, which began in April and lasted until the first part of July, had its origins in a disagreement between the government and the miners over a wage readjustment approved in October 1972. The opposition declared strong support for the workers even though their demands meant salary increases which far exceeded those of other workers. Though it must be noted that much of the support for the strike came from the professional unions, the strike had a demoralizing effect on the government and divided the workers. Other workers, such as the miners of Chuquicamata, declared "solidarity strikes" with those of El Teniente. At Chuquicamata, a motion supported by white-collar workers won. Blue-collar workers continued to work in extraordinarily difficult circumstances. The strike demonstrated further the essentially economic demands of the elite groups of the working class and their lack of strong revolutionary consciousness.
29. See *Ercilla*, 13–19 June 1973, pp. 7–10. For an article sharply critical of the court, see Victor Vaccaro, "Escándalo en la Corte," *Chile Hoy*, 22–28 June, pp. 16–17. The exchange of letters between the president and the court has already been cited. See n. 3.
30. That Allende was intent on pursuing a dialogue, and that the Christian Democrats, and Frei in particular, were not interested, is also evidenced by some "behind the scenes" developments. In May, Allende sought, through the good offices of the cardinal, to set up a personal conversation with Frei to discuss the serious crisis. Frei refused to participate in any private meeting with the president, arguing that he would only attend a public meeting following a public invitation. Frei did not trust the president. He would not consider the possibility that Allende was making a genuine effort to resolve the country's difficulties and refused to recognize that Allende, like himself, was under enormous political pressures from his own camp. That Allende was even willing to risk a private meeting set up at his initiative is evidence of good faith. These observations, and the section on the Christian Democratic convention, are based on extensive interviews primarily with prominent Christian Democrats.
31. The fragment that retained the strongest claim to a party's traditions had a much better chance of surviving. Both the MAPU and the Izquierda Cristiana, though taking with them important leadership elements of the party, were not able to retain support at the polls. The same was true with the fragments of the Radical party, the Democracia Radical and the Partido de Izquierda Radical, or the fragment of the Socialist party, the Union Socialista Popular. In the 1973 congressional elections the minor parties and all segments of the divided Radical party fared very poorly.
32. According to prominent members of the progressive faction of the Christian Democratic party, in interviews with the author, one of Allende's principal mistakes was not to try to be more accommodating toward the Christian Democratic party during the early years of his

administration. The progressive wing of the party still controlled the party leadership and a defection of the Right might have been possible. This would have been to the advantage of both the government and the leftist and centrist elements in the Christian Democrats. A split, after the leadership had been taken over by the more conservative wing of the party, would act only to the detriment of the more moderate sectors, who would risk becoming politically insignificant.

33. *Chile Hoy*, 6–12 July 1973, p. 11.
34. Ibid.
35. Ibid.
36. Quoted by Regis Debray in "Il es mort dans sa loi," *Le Nouvel Observateur*, no. 462 (17–23 September 1973), p. 37.
37. In interviews with the author, leaders of the Christian Democrats and top officials of the Allende government who were involved in the negotiations concurred with this assessment. They noted that while the air force and the navy might have been ready to move, the army was divided enough that a compromise would have made it difficult to get the vital army support for military action. This is very important. Leaders on both sides were not convinced that a coup was inevitable. And even in retrospect they speculated that it could have been averted as of July 1973. They (particularly the leadership of the Christian Democrats) did not realize at the time that the lack of compromise was in itself an important catalyst for the coup.
38. *Ercilla*, 18–24 July 1973, p. 7.
39. Ibid.
40. *Chile Hoy*, 13–19 July 1973, p. 8.
41. Ibid., p. 6.
42. *Chile Hoy,* 6–12 July 1973, p. 3.
43. This and succeeding sections are also based in part on interviews with former high-level political leaders, primarily Christian Democrats.
44. The statement can be found in Echeverría and Frei, *La lucha por la juricidad*, vol. 3, pp. 123–24. It is instructive that the day of the coup attempt the leadership of the Christian Democratic party met for hours and was unable to decide on an official reaction until after the insurrection had failed.
45. *Ercilla*, 11–17 July 1973, p. 9.
46. This section is based on interviews with Gabriel Valdés in February and March 1974. It was corroborated in interviews with other principals who were at the dinner. Private conversation between the president and C.D. officials were actually officially prohibited by the C.D. leadership, which feared reaction from the Nationals and C.D. supporters.
47. The press carried good accounts of the conversations. This section, however, relies primarily on interviews. For a published account, see *Ercilla*, 8–14 August 1973, pp. 7–10.
48. See the special supplement to *El Mercurio* published on 11 September 1974 entitled "Como llegaron las fuerzas armadas a la acción del 11 de Septiembre de 1973." The author of the twenty-four-page supplement, Arturo Fontaine Aldunate, the associate director of the newspaper, interviewed at length "more than fifteen" high-ranking officers who were "first line protagonists." Despite the fact that the account is self-serving and that Fontaine does not hide his own biases, this report is extraordinarily valuable because it paints a full picture of the gradual move toward a military coup in the three services, particularly in the navy. Another useful, though less informative account based on very well-placed sources is the article by William Montalbano, "How the Chilean Military Toppled Allende," in the *Miami Herald*, 16 September 1973, pp. 1, 22A.
49. For the slogans see *Chile Hoy*, 6–12 July 1973, p. 15.
50. We know that some officers were conspiring from the beginning. Several conspirators were removed in the wake of the Schneider assassination and internal incidents within the armed forces in later periods, such as September 1972. The CIA successfully "penetrated" one group of plotters in January of 1972. The CIA received reports on the group planning a coup through July, August, and September of 1973. See Select Committee on Intelligence, U.S. Senate, "Covert Action in Chile," p. 39. The point is not that plotting did not exist, but rather that the process through which the plotters had to go in order to move the institution toward a coup was a long and tedious one.

51. See Fontaine, "Como llegaron las fuerzas armadas," p.10.
52. In an earlier version of this study, I argued that intervention by Allende in the hierarchy of rank was one of the factors which contributed to military dissatisfaction. Since the writing of that work I have been able to conduct further interviews with high-ranking officials in the Allende government. On the basis of those interviews and a reevaluation of the public record, it seems that the question of disturbance of the hierarchy of rank by the president was not an important one. In fact, Allende scrupulously resisted efforts by many people in his own coalition to obtain more loyal officers. See, for example, the letter by Senator Altamirano to Allende in which the Socialist leader threatened to withdraw the minister of the interior from the cabinet unless the president finally agreed to replace some leaders of the Carabineros. The letter, ironically, is published in the Junta de Gobierno, *Libro blanco del cambio de gobierno en Chile* (Santiago: Editorial Lord Cochrane, 1973), p. 113, as purported evidence of Popular Unity meddling in the armed forces. As will be clear below, it was not only the Socialist who wanted officers replaced; the plotters also wanted the president to move down the hierarchy of rank to ensure the success of their plans. The earlier study is "Il crollo della democrazia in Chile," *Revista Italiana di Scienza Politica* 5, no. 1 (April 1975): 83–129.
53. See the article by Faride Zerán, "El poder popular en acción," *Chile Hoy*, 6–12 July 1973, pp. 6–7. This was one of a multitude of articles which appeared after the coup celebrating the potential of working-class mobilization to fend off a coup by occupation of factories and even armed resistance. For a treatment of the *comandos comunales*, see "Comandos comunales: Órganos de Poder del Pueblo," *Punto Final*, no. 189 (31 July 1973).
54. *Chile Hoy*, 13–19 July 1973, p. 8.
55. Ibid., p. 6.
56. Ibid., p. 7.
57. MAPU Garretón faction, *Boletín Informativo*, no. 5.
58. Despite the enormous publicity to the cordones, they never constituted a massive force. When the government sought to return industries taken over by workers in the attempted coup, many workers resisted. At one point the Cordón Los Cerrillos barricaded themselves inside factories to prevent the devolution of industries. Though perhaps five thousand workers were mobilized, that number was a small fraction of the Santiago working class. In interviews with the author, a sociologist from the University of Chile who was working closely with the Cordón Los Cerrillos put the active members at only a few hundred. The account by Patricia Santa Lucia, "The Industrial Working Class and the Struggle for Power in Chile," in *Allende's Chile*, ed. Philip O'Brien (New York: Praeger Special Studies in International Politics and Government, 1976), pp. 128–66, which paints a picture of a strong movement in the text, reveals the weakness of the cordones in an appendix which attempts to list cordones and their membership.
59. Allende and the Communist party understood this and through their control of the Central Unica de Trabajadores sought to downplay the cordones after an initial period of praise. In turn they left themselves open to charges that they were unwilling to let the working class defend itself. It is clear to this author, however, that there was no way in which the working class could have been mobilized to fight and die in such a short period of time, given the essentially economic outlook of the great bulk of the population and the escalating conspiracy in the armed forces. The maximalist Left was engaged in a self-fulfilling prophecy.
60. On these plans, see Fontaine, "Como llegaron las fuerzas armadas," p. 11. Prats signed the documents.
61. *Chile Hoy*, 3–10 July 1973, p. 8. These statements incensed military leaders; see William Montaldo, "How the Chilean Military Toppled Allende."
62. *Ercilla*, 5–11 August 1973, pp. 7–8.
63. This is derived from conversations with cabinet officers close to Allende. See also Regis Debray, "Il est mort dans sa loi," p. 37.
64. It is quite clear that the strikers were not willing to settle for any satisfaction of their immediate economic demands; they were intent on forcing the president to resign from office or provoking a coup. This view of the strikers' intent was shared by prominent Christian Democrats who spoke out publicly. See Renán Fuentealba's interview in *Chile Hoy*, 17–23 August 1973, p. 28. At this same time the Forty Committee in Washington approved another

$1 million to support opposition groups. The money was not spent as the coup was imminent. See Select Committee on Intelligence, U.S. Senate, "Covert Action in Chile," p. 61.

65. In interviews and correspondence with the author, President Frei strongly denied that he was involved in any coup attempt. It is clear, however, that President Frei thought that a coup was imminent, and more importantly, inevitable, It is also clear that he did have direct contacts with some officers, including his former military aides Generals Bonilla and Arellano. Some of his closest associates, Sergio Ossa and Juan de Dios Carmona, had close ties with military officers and probably knew of the impending coup. This author doubts that the former president was directly involved in any conspiracy. Nevertheless, by his inaction he tacitly supported the coup. Frei was the most important political figure in the opposition and along with Allende the most prominent politican in the country. Had he used his influence to oppose a coup, both privately and publicly, it would have made it extremely difficult for the military to act. Some of Frei's colleagues sensed that. Only ten days before the coup Bernardo Leighton, his former minister of the interior and an old friend who maintained contacts with Allende, urged Frei to talk to Allende in an effort to stave off the coup. Frei once again argued that he would only talk to Allende publicly, failing to appreciate that the situation in September 1973 was very different from what it had been in May of that year when he set down similar conditions. The declaration issued by the Christian Democrats after the coup reflected the thinking of Frei and the leadership. It blamed the government exclusively for the situation in Chile and noted that the armed forces "did not seek power" and that "their institutional traditions and the republican history of the country inspires confidence that as soon as the tasks which they have assumed to avoid the grave dangers of destruction and totalitarianism which threatened the Chilean nation have been completed, they will return power to the sovereign people." When several Christian Democrats, including Bernardo Leighton, issued a public declaration condemning the coup, Frei went out of his way, in an interview with *ABC* magazine, to argue that that group represented a minority in the party and that the military had "saved Chile." The Christian Democratic declaration, that of those who opposed the coup, and a summary of Frei's *ABC* interview can be found in *Chile-America*, no. 4 (1975), pp. 43–49.

That a bold attempt by politicians to avert a coup would have received significant popular support is evidenced by a survey taken in Santiago only days before the coup. Fifty-one and one-half percent of the respondents thought the military should not involve itself in the political sphere, compared to only 27.5 percent who thought it should. The authors of the poll concluded that despite the fact that 72 percent of the sample as opposed to a mere 3 percent thought the country was living in "abnormal times," Chileans still preferred a "democratic solution." For the survey see *Ercilla*, 22–28 August 1973, pp. 18–19.

66. The Chamber's resolution argued, among other things, that from the beginning the Allende government had sought to gain total power, that in so doing it had violated the constitution and laws and had ignored other powers, particularly Congress. It called on the military cabinet members, by virtue of their oath of loyalty to the constitution, to "place an immediate end to all situations referred to that infringe the constitution and laws, in order to channel governmental action through lawful paths and assure constitutional order for our fatherland and the essential bases of democratic conviviality among Chileans." Allende in answering the congressional action noted that it would "facilitate the seditious intentions of certain sectors . . .the deputies of oppositon formally exhorted the Armed Forces and Police to adopt a deliberating posture with respect to executive power, and break their duty to obey the Supreme Government. . . ." See Echeverría and Frei, *La lucha por la juricidad,* vol. 3, pp. 199–211. Allende had tried to stave off the vote in the Chamber. Orlando Letelier pleaded to no avail with Bernardo Leighton to try to stop the vote. Later, both Leighton and Tomic would point to the action of the Chamber as one of the major mistakes of the Christian Democratic party.

67. See Fontaine, "Como llegaron las fuerzas armadas," for the fascinating narrative.

68. On the Communist party position see the summary of a forthcoming book by Eduardo Labarca reported in *Chile-America*, nos. 12–13 (November-December 1975), pp. 75–77.

69. See Fontaine, "Come llegaron las fuerzas armadas," p. 20.

70. The military, however, did go to some length to try to ensure cohesiveness in the armed forces. Shortly after the coup it was announced that the armed forces had moved to prevent

the government from carrying out a Z plan which called for the assassination of a host of military officers during the 19 September 1973 military parade. And yet, according to military spokesmen themselves, the Z plan was only discovered after the coup. Whether the plan was actually one of many plans undoubtedly produced by a host of little groups (this Z plan called for the assassination of Allende himself, thus also raising questions about the military's view that the government was preparing the action), or a fabrication, it was used to instill fear in the army. Top leaders of the Christian Democratic party who supported the military coup when it took place told the author that they had little doubt that the Z plan was a fabrication. For the Z plan, see the official publication which the junta put out shortly after the coup in order to justify their actions, *Libro blanco del cambio de gobierno en Chile*. An English-language version was published and widely disseminated in the United States. According to the U.S. Senate Committee on Intelligence, the CIA paid the travel expenses of pro-junta spokesmen who went abroad to support the military action. See "Covert Action in Chile," pp. 40, 62. In interviews with the author, other participants and observers of the period shortly after the coup also interpreted the severity of the repression as a mechanism used by the armed forces to ensure loyalty. Even on Dawson Island, where there was clearly no possibility of attack, the military was kept in constant fear of an imminent attack. According to one military officer who fled the country shortly after the coup, General Oscar Bonilla had to work hard on 10 September to obtain the loyalty of many officers. See *Chile-America*, no. 5 (31 March 1975), p. 24.

71. For a discussion of over thirty works that have appeared since and reflect previous and current thinking on the Chilean experience by a cross-section of authors, see Arturo Valenzuela and Samuel Valenzuela, "Visions of Chile," *Latin American Research Review* 10, no. 3: 155–75.

Index

Abdication of moderates, 96, 107–8. *See also* Center agreement

Agrarian reform, 9, 16; under Allende, 121 n, 153 n; constraints on, 115 n; under Frei, 29, 36; and unionization under Allende, 29, 53, 117 n

Alessandri, Jorge, 7, 8, 34; and 1970 elections, 37, 39, 40–44, 119 n. *See also* Alessandri, Jorge, government of

Alessandri, Jorge, government of, 7, 20, 23–24, 25, 34

Allende, Salvador: ambivalent posture of, 89, 107; and approval of moderate ministry, 95–96; and difficulties of coalition management, 65, 68, 88; and exchange of letters with officials, 91–92; and isolation of, 105, 129–30 n; and military, 82, 86–88, 93, 98, 103; as national figure, 8; and 1970 election, 39–43; options of, after 1973 election, 86–88, 97, 105; and problem of violence, 69; and split with socialists, 94, 97, 103; strategy of, as minority one, 48; and Via Chilena stand, 43–44, 118 n; and views on constitutional amendment, 73. *See also* Allende, Salvador, government of

Allende, Salvador, government of: and agrarian reform, 115 n, 121 n; and bargaining attempts in 1973, 95–98; and economic difficulties, 54–58, 61–64, 123 n; economic policy of, 50–56, 64; and foreign aid, 56; ideological splits within, 66–68, 123 n; and need for Christian Democratic support, 70; and 1971 election, 53–54, 58; and problem of violence, 68–69; program of, 50. *See also* Allende, Salvador; Communist party; Popular Unity; Socialist party

Almeyda, Clodomiro, 95

Almond, Gabriel, 33

Altamirano, Carlos, 84, 94, 102, 119 n, 128 n, 131 n

Angell, Alan, 33

Antidemocratic movements. *See* Disloyal groups

Area de Propiedad Social, Ley sobre. *See* Social property, law on

Arellano, Sergio, 109, 132 n

Arena, narrowing of, 92–93, 97, 105

Armed forces, 20–21; de facto control of state, 98; and the election of 1973, 83; and fear of insubordination, 102–3; and fear of parallel army, 100–102; foreign aid to, 127 n; government of, 107–10; as mediators, 65, 82–83; neglect of, 20; as neutral powers, 82–83; and the October 1972 strike, 82; opposition to ENU, 89–90; policy of U.P. toward, 82; politization of, 83, 88; and repression, 107; struggle within, 88, 91, 98–99; and 29 June coup attempt, 99. *See also* Coups d'etat, attempted

Arming the people, 94, 95, 100–103

Arms Control Law, 101–2

Aylwin, Patricio, 91, 92, 96–97

Balance of Trade: before Allende, 19–25; in 1971–72, 55

Baltra, Alberto, 47

Banco Central de Chile (Central Bank), 16, 51, 64

Banco del Estado de Chile (State Bank), 16

Bitar, Sergio, 114 n

Black market, 55–56

Blest, Clotario, 29

Bonilla, Oscar, 104, 132 n, 133 n

135